Feeling Hopeless? Learn How to Talk So Your Kids Will Listen in 2021

2021 Most Updated Exercises and Best

Practices

Adam E. Smith

contained within this document, including, but not limited to, errors, omissions, or inaccuracies.

Table of Contents

Introduction

It is perhaps a no-brainer that it is difficult for any parent to develop a strong relationship with their children. Throughout history, there has been a well-known resistance in the understanding between a parent and their child.

Although the different stresses brought on by the state of the world can negatively affect the relationship between you and your child, the conflict between parent and child, according to experts, generally stems from a lack of communication between the pair. On the one hand, this comes from the child's desire to test the limits of their parents' power and develop their own independence; on the other hand, this resistance comes from the parent's desire to protect their child and help them to become a strong independent person and adult.

Parents around the world and throughout history have struggled to find guides and tips to help build stronger communication between themselves and their children. However, many child psychologists and specialists have come up with collections of lists that are said to help parents do everything from disciplining their children to connecting on their level. Nevertheless, with each year or so brings with it a new set of world issues that makes parenting harder. Most recently, in the years of 2020 and 2121, parents have been given the additional challenges of working from home, having their children be homeschooled, and generally having to navigate a pandemic.

This book is designed to help guide you through the challenges of communication with your children, and come out the other side with a stronger and closer relationship with your child or children. To do so this book has been divided into three general parts and sections, each holding their own smaller chapters. These sections will highlight and focus on three important aspects of developing a stronger communication and relationship with your child.

Listening

This book focuses on the skill of listening first, as you must be able to listen to your child—and conversely have them listen to you—in order to communicate better with each other. The first chapter explores the different theories and aspects of listening. Essentially, the first chapter will state what is needed in order for an individual to listen and what it means to do so properly. The second chapter moves from the theories of listening to how to get your children to listen to you. This chapter will make suggestions of how to encourage your children to listen and include different exercises that can increase their skill to listen. The last chapter in this first section will make a shift from getting your kids to listen to you to getting you to listen to your kids. Listening goes both ways in communication; you cannot expect your child to listen to you when you do not show them that you care about what they say and communicate.

Communication

The second section of this book will focus on the communication, that is the message sharing, aspect of building a better relationship between you and your child. The first chapter again talks about the philosophy and theories behind how message sharing and communication works generally speaking. By understanding how communication and message sharing works, you can better understand why it fails at times, allowing you to perhaps understand why there is a breakdown in communication between you and your child. Keeping with the theme and pattern of the above sections, the following two chapters in this second section will focus on how to talk to your kids in a way that they will be reciprocal to it, and how to get your kids to talk to you about different issues and aspects of their life, respectively.

Understanding

One last aspect of how to better communicate with your child is to try and understand their point of view and what they are going through that may be negatively affecting your relationship with them. This aspect of understanding is what the third and final section of this book will focus on. The first chapter will explore, gently and sensitively, the different issues and stresses that children often experience that are discredited and disregarded by adults. The second chapter will focus on the aspects of being a parent that most every parent dreads: punishment and discipline. Although punishing and disciplining your child is a very taboo subject, as different methods are considered inappropriate, it is still a necessary part of raising children. For this reason, this chapter will focus on how to discipline your child in a way that they understand the consequences—using methods that discipline and educate rather than are punishment focused. The last chapter in this section and the book as whole will focus on the external factor that can affect the relationship with your child. Specifically, this chapter will make reference to how the current state of the world may be affecting your relationship.

Furthermore, keeping with the conceptual thread of the relationship being strained due to the stressful and ever-changing situation happening in the world right now, the issues and exercises to mend and strengthen the relationship that will be suggested within these pages will be focused on the difficulties that have been experienced due to the current state of the world.

Following the conclusion of this book, there will be a few different help guides that will include different exercises and activities to help improve your relationship. These help guides, although not containing new information, will elaborate on the activities suggested within the chapters to act as quick reference forms.

Ultimately, this book will give you the tools and the motivation needed to improve and mend the relationship between you and your child.

Part 1:

Listening

Chapter 1:

Theories Behind Listening

Perhaps the first complaint that many parents have when it comes to inability to create or develop a strong relationship with their child is that their child simply does not listen to them. In order to explain and understand why it may seem like your child is simply not listening, and to understand better how you can improve the listening portion of your relationship, you must first understand how listening works.

Hearing vs. Listening

The distinction that must be made in understanding how listening works is to differentiate between hearing and listening. Hearing is simply a physical response sensing something with your ears or auditory senses. For example, you can hear a train go by, you can hear someone talking but not discern what they're saying, or you can hear a bump in the night but not understand what it is. Lastly, you can hear the word someone is saying however not necessarily understand what they are saying. In general, hearing is the physical sensation of using your auditory senses.

On the other hand, listening is much more involved. Listening is a cognitive and physical action taken on the part of the person as they are taking in the information that is being sensed audibly, evaluating the information and understanding the information. In this way, listening is a skill or a talent that must be developed by each and every individual. Where hearing may be an unconscious, natural, and automatic physical response, listening takes practice to do properly (Kline, 1996).

Process of Listening

Another way to differentiate between hearing and listening is that the process of listening requires much more cognitive ability than hearing does. Generally, there are six steps that the individual must go through in order to be considered listening. By name they are receiving, selecting, interpreting, understanding, evaluating, and resolving, which will be explained below (Klien, 1996):

- Receiving

The first step in the listening process is receiving. The listener, or intended listener that is, must first get this stimuli. Auditory information must be sent from one person or thing to the intended receiver and that receiver, or in other words the intended listener, must be able to physically hear the stimuli. If the listener cannot receive or acknowledge the auditory stimuli then, right off the bat, the listening process is compromised.

This first part of the listening process is the step that is as closely linked to hearing as possible. This is because the receiving step is the physical response and sense of the ear. There is very little critical thinking response needed for this first step of the listening process to be successful.

- Selecting

The next step in the listening process is at the end of the visual, the person must select what part of the auditory information is important, and therefore requires them to focus on it. When an individual is hearing someone talking, listening to music, or receiving any sort of audible information, there is a variety of different auditory stimuli that is being received. Furthermore, there might be competing auditory stimuli reaching for the attention of the intended listener. Therefore, the listener, in order to listen properly, must select which audible stimuli and which part of the audible stimuli they wish to focus on.

For example, are they trying to isolate the drum beat of a song rather than the vocal melody? Are they trying to listen to the words of someone's message or sentence rather than their accent? Ultimately, for this next step of the listening process to be successful, the intended listener must be able to differentiate between audible stimuli, its parts, and which part of the stimuli is most important.

This step in the listening process requires both a physical response and a critical thinking response from the listener.

- Interpreting

The third step to the listening process is interpreting the audible stimuli. This step requires the individual to attach meaning to the audible stimuli. For instance, if they hear the whistle of a train, this step is what attaches the name train to the sound.

This step involves the individual searching their memory and past experiences to discover which of their past knowledge best fits with the audible stimuli that they are receiving in the moment. Of course, this step does not happen consciously, nor does it happen through an extraneous process. Usually this map of interpretation happens automatically for the individual as they hear a stimulus and automatically associated with a concept, a meaning, or an idea that they have previously collected.

In fact, the interpretation process only becomes noticeable when the individual does not have a matching concept or meaning to the immediate audible stimuli.

- Understanding

The next step in the listening process is understanding interpretation and the audible stimulus itself. This is closely linked to the interpretation field as they usually happen simultaneously or consecutively.

Generally, the understanding step of this process means that the individual—the listener—is able to place the different meanings and messages that are being received into their larger framework of knowledge. Again, this requires the individual to revive past experiences in order to match up with the current stimuli.

- Evaluating

The evaluation step of the listening process is when the individual takes the whole of the different individual audible stimuli—that is the different words and sounds that they hear—and evaluates them into one generalized meaning.

For example, in the interpretation and understanding steps of the listening process, the individual is taking each individual word and sound as its own entity and matching it with a meaning or concept previously learned. In the evaluation step, the individual is taking the entirety of the sounds, or the entire sentence said by the other individual, in order to draw from it the generalized meaning the other in person is trying to communicate.

However, the evaluation step of the listening process is the individual judging what the meaning of the audible stimuli is. This step of the process, although based on the information brought in by the physical sense of hearing, is largely based in the mind of the person.

- Resolving

The last and final step of the listening process is the resolving or the resolution stop. In this step, the individual decides what to do with the information given and how the information can be useful to them. That is where the individual decides whether or not they will use the information provided. It is also in this stage where the listener will discern between the intention and goal of the person who is speaking or the other audible stimuli in the first place.

Lastly, this is also the stage where the individual is able to decide whether or not further information will be needed in order to fully understand the message of the speaker, or the noise maker.

* * *

Therefore, in order for an individual to listen effectively, they must move through the aforementioned six steps. Of course, these steps do not necessarily happen consciously nor does the listener necessarily have to be aware of each step happening. Ideally, the listening process happens automatically and subconsciously.

However, for those individuals who are trying to improve their listening skills, they may want to actively pay attention to each step, in order to isolate which step of the process is providing the most obstacle or hindrance to their listening skills (Klien, 1996).

Different Types of Listening

Although the process of listening is always the same, there are different types of listening that an individual can participate in. These different types of listening really come into play within the last two steps of the listening process; however, the context of the different types of listening will most often be present for the individual to be aware of before the listening takes place.

Appreciative Listening

The first type of listening is appreciative listening. This type is when the individual enjoys what they are listening to. This type is usually sought out for enjoyment; the individual chooses things that make them happy to listen to. That is not to say that the individual cannot make a shift to appreciative listening from another type.

This type of listening can be when you are listening to music or watching a show that you like. It can also be listening to a person that you enjoy listening to. Any type of listening that ignites joy, happiness, or enjoyment is appreciative listening.

The appreciative listening is usually connected to what the person values or what their hobbies are. If someone enjoys hiking, then their appreciative listening will most likely be the sounds of nature; whereas someone whose hobby is reading may experience appreciative listening and will be more silent to allow them to read.

Empathic Listening

This second type of listening is present when you are listening to something that invokes a sense of concern, empathy, or sympathy from the listener. Instances and examples when empathic listening is present is when you are listening to a distraught family member or friend. This type of listening can also be present when you are listening to a concerned news report or hear of a distressing situation.

Ultimately, empathic listening is the type that brings out emotions of empathy and concern from the listener. Individuals who perhaps are not skilled or practiced in this type of listening are usually those individuals that are not receptive to empathy or concern themselves with it. Therefore, they are unable to recognize when they must feel and show concern or empathy.

Comprehensive or Informative Listening

Comprehensive or informative listening is the type of listening that is present when you are trying to understand what is being presented to you. This type of listening is found most often in schools where there are many individuals and students that are trying to learn different subjects. However, perhaps a more subtle example of comprehensive listening, is also present when the individual is talking to someone else who is trying to explain a concept to another.

This type of listening requires the individual to know and understand that they are trying to learn or understand something. Therefore, individuals who perhaps find it more difficult to admit that they do not know something will most often be bad at this type of listening.

Critical Listening

This fourth type of listening is listening that is present when judgements are required. Not to be confused with comprehensive or informative listening, critical listening is when the auditory stimuli posits a question or a problem to the listener. For example, when you are listening to someone who has a different opinion than you, or you are listening to a news report that strikes you as problematic or stressful.

In these situations, there is a moment of reflection that takes place where the listener judges their own opinion and value of what they just heard. For this reason, critical listening can also be used as a defense mechanism to discern what noises and sounds are threatening and which are not.

Individuals who have more critical thinking skills may need more practice in this type of listening over others.

Discriminative Listening

The last type of listening is discriminative or discriminatory listening. This listening is employed when you are trying to differentiate between different sounds and their meanings. Similar but not the same as critical listening, this type of listening is when you are faced with many different sounds and auditory stimuli that you must differentiate between which sounds belong to which source, or which meaning belongs to which stimuli.

This type of listening also becomes useful when you are faced with different information or different opinions at one time. It is the discriminative listening skills that allows individuals to form judgements about the meaning behind different audible stimuli.

Individuals who tend to become overwhelmed easily may not be skilled at this type of listening, as they may not be able to focus on a specific meaning or auditory stimuli.

Therefore, generally speaking, the four types of listening are really based on the situation at hand. Is the auditory stimuli coming from someone who is trying to share information? Is the information coming from someone who is trying to prove a point? Or, again, is the stimuli something from the outside world that is trying to get your attention?

What is important to note is that each situation does not ask for only one type of listening. Rather, each situation can involve many different types of listening types, and the listening type can change and shift as the auditory stimuli changes. For example, discriminative and critical listening can be used in times of survival to discern threatening noises. On the other hand, appreciative listening can be used if you are in school and you enjoy what you are listening to.

Individuals who are skilled at listening are able to automatically discern between the types of listening that is being asked for within the different situations (Kline, 1996).

One more important aspect of these types of listening is that the above list is not necessarily exhaustive. Over the years, experts and academics have shortened this list to only three types of listening, only to then expand the list to include up to 10 types. The above five types were chosen as they are the five that show up the most often.

When Does Listening Fail?

Based on the parts of the listening process, and different types of listening, one can deduce how the listening process can fail. Namely, it fails when either the person or thing that is creating the audible stimuli or the receiver of the audible stimuli is compromised in some way (Grohol, 2016).

Of course, there are a plethora of specific reasons as to why listening fails; that is to say there are many reasons as to why the stimuli or the receiver of the listening process can be compromised. Out of the very long list, the following are five reasons that listening can fail that are perhaps the most often applied or found in situations between a parent and a child (Grohol, 2016):

Defensiveness

The first reason as to why listening may fail is because the listener may be defensive. Defensiveness is an emotional reaction that is invoked when the individual senses that there is a threat to their emotional or mental well-being.

At times, an individual who is listening to another speak may become defensive when the other speaks of something that they disagree with. This could stem from either a personal opinion, a fact, or a comment that is directly meant to put the listener on their heels.

When the listener becomes defensive in their ability to understand, evaluate the information that they are receiving. This is because as a defense mechanism, rather than pulling up instances and examples of knowledge that match the audible stimuli, their brain will pull up knowledge to counteract the stimulus to ensure that their knowledge base and beliefs do not change.

Personal Prejudice and Bias

Similarly to defensiveness, personal bias and prejudice can hinder the listening process by the way of the listener. Each person has a certain set of beliefs and knowledge that are hardwired into their brain. These biases then manipulate the lens through which the individual sees the world. To be clear, these biases do not necessarily have to be prejudice about race or culture. The biases and prejudices that affect listening can be as simple as believing that orange juice is better than apple juice.

In this way, personal prejudice—that is the strong beliefs of an individual that close their mind off to other beliefs—negatively impacts the listening process, as the individual will be less likely to accept, understand, and evaluate what they are hearing in a positive way.

The prejudices do not have to be in place only when another individual is talking. Rather, the listener can have their prejudices affect their listening process when it comes to natural sounds, as well. For example, if the individual were to hear a sound, one that is abstract and from an unknown source that does not match the visual scenery around them, their prejudice or bias about what is to be expected in terms of audible census will tell them that the noise did not belong to their environment. This becomes problematic when the noise, that the individual based on their bias ignored, is one that is warning them of danger.

In saying all of that, however, personal biases and prejudices are often found mostly in conversations with other individuals.

Being Preoccupied

Another factor that can lead to a fail in listening, especially when it comes to children and parents listening to each other, is when the listener is preoccupied. Preoccupation is when you are physically and or mentally busy with many things at the same time. When it comes to listening, preoccupation comes into play, as it distracts the individual from participating in the proper listening process.

Preoccupation, that is for example doing something else while your child is talking to you, hinders your ability to listen by affecting everything from whether or not you are able to accept the auditory stimuli to whether or not you are able to understand and evaluate information. Furthermore, being preoccupied can also lead to a lack of patience and understanding in the listening process.

Alternatively, it is important to ensure that your child is not preoccupied when you are trying to talk to them as the results can be the same.

Not Being Interested

Another hindrance to the listening process is when the listener is not interested in the audible stimuli. Similar to being preoccupied, not being interested in what is being presented to you may allow your mind to wander and be distracted by other things, thereby blocking or negatively affecting your ability to hear the audible stimuli properly.

As a parent, it may be difficult to stay interested in what your child is saying, but it is important to show them that showing interest in what is being said to them will help them listen better. Furthermore, by understanding that being interested in what is being heard is an important aspect of the listening process, you can change how you speak to your children to ensure that their interest remains.

Mistrust of the Other

One last factor that goes into failed listening is when the listener does not trust the source of the sound. If the listener does not trust the source of the sound or audible stimuli, then their integration, understanding, and following steps in the listening process are compromised.

Similar to how personal biases and defensiveness hinders the listening process, not trusting the source of the sound makes the listener question everything that follows. If it is a natural sound, then not trusting the source can confuse the individual about their surroundings and allow them to miss an important aspect of their environment. On the other hand, if the sound is a conversation and the source is another person that the listener distrusts, then they are likely to not pay attention, follow up, or give credit to what they hear.

* * *

As previously stated, these are not the only ways in which listening can fail. They were chosen because these are the ways that listening is usually compromised in the relationship of parent and child. Through these five different explanations as to why your child is perhaps not listening, it can be seen and understood that children who do not listen have much more going on than simply not wanting to listen (Grohol, 2016).

Chapter 2:

How to Get Your Kids to Listen to

You

Following from the above theories of listening, there comes to light one clear role: the listener. The listener is the person who is accepting the auditory stimuli; the listener is the person to whom the auditory stimuli is projected toward.

However, when it comes to the auditory stimuli of conversations, there is another important role: the speaker.

Unfortunately, when it comes to listening, the responsibility and blame of the failure to listen falls on the listener. This is because it is considered their responsibility to ensure that they are paying attention to their surroundings and to the message that is being shared. Based on this biased yet accepted belief that it is the responsibility of the child to listen, many parents get frustrated and angry with their children when they do not listen. This is because the parents believe that their child is purposefully not listening. However this is not necessarily the case. Listening is a skill and talent that must be developed. Therefore, it could be the case that your child has yet obtained this skill which is the reason behind why they seem to not listen to you (McCready, n.d.).

Of course, as the parent, the responsibility then falls on you to help your child develop the skill of listening which can be a daunting task when not tackled properly. Teaching your child anything requires patience, time, and listening—the skill you are trying to teach them.

This makes your problems and teaching philosophy slightly circular. Your child needs to listen in order to better develop and improve their listening skills. What makes this task most challenging, and frustrating, is that when you try to teach a young child anything, they are likely to push back and become frustrated themselves when they feel as though they are not being successful.

Thankfully, child development experts, including pediatricians and child psychologists, have developed a list of suggestions and tips to help you teach your child to develop their listening skills, without pressuring them to do so (Positive Parenting, 2021).

The following is a list of ways that can help your child listen to you. For each suggestion there will be a discussion of how the suggestion will help and which reason for not listening it can counteract.

Get on Their Level

The first way to get your children to listen to you is to get on their level. Your child lives their lives looking up to everyone they meet in a dramatically physical sense. Other than their friends and schoolmates, everyone your child meets is much taller than them. This is an intimidating way to live. When voices get louder, this intimidation gets more intense. For this reason, your child may naturally feel as though they have to defend themselves against whoever is talking to them, putting them on the defensive and being too scared to listen to the words you are saying.

To counteract this, it is suggested that you physically get onto your child's level. This means to crouch, kneel, or bend so you are able to look your child in their eye. Even if, when you kneel, you are lower than your child that is okay. By getting down to their physical level, or lower, you are ridding the situation of the intimidation that you child may feel. By getting down to their level, you are also pulling their focus onto you which increases the chances of your child listening to you. Lastly, by bringing our face to their level, you are also limiting the chances of your yelling or raising your temper; it is difficult to shout and yell when you are crouching.

Altogether, kneeling and bringing yourself down to your child's level is the first step to helping your child listen to you better.

Don't Use Don't

Another way to get your kids to listen to you is to avoid using the word "don't." "Don't" is an aggressive negative word that assumes the individual was about to do an action that must be warned against. For example, when you tell someone "don't do that," you are warning them to not act in a way that you assume they will.

For example, you see your child running toward the couch and you say, "Don't jump on the couch!" With this, you are assuming that your child will behave badly. Therefore, by using the word "don't" repeatedly, your child may begin to resist the word as they feel as though you do not trust their judgment in behavior.

Therefore, rather than using this word, try to rephrase your statement, suggestion, or request in a positive way. By doing, so your child will feel as though you were asking them to do you a positive favor rather than considering you to be controlling their actions and behaviors. If we take, for example, your child running to the couch and instead of using a phrase with "don't" in it, try using the phrase "remember to sit nice, please."

With this simple rephrasing you are changing the tone of your request to a positive one from a negative one. This is very important to remember because when children are young, and are learning what words mean, they rely heavily on tone. Therefore, if your tone is one that is constantly negative, they are more likely to act in a way that disobeys your request.

Say Yes

Another way to help your child listen more, that is similar to the above suggestion, is rather than saying "no" all the time, say "yes." Similar to the negative effects of the word "don't," the word "no" can lead your child to believing that you do not trust in their judgment nor their actions. This may lead them to act in a disobedient or poor way. Saying "yes" will turn your request and answer into a tone that is positive.

To be clear, saying "yes" does not mean that you have to agree with, say "yes" to, or allow your child to do anything they want. Rather, rephrase your "no" into a positive and "yes" like phrase.

For example, if your child repeatedly asks to have chocolate before dinner and you find yourself constantly saying "no," you may find your child is sneaking chocolate or candy without your permission. Therefore, try saying "yes, but you can have it after dinner." Using a phrase such as this, you are giving the child the "yes" they want, but you are controlling the situation in the way you want.

Do Not Lecture

It is important that when your child does not listen to you, and they perhaps get hurt or break something, that you do not lecture them about how you told them not to act in such a way or about the consequences.

If some sort of negative consequence has come from an action or behavior that you warned against, there is a good chance that your child is already feeling shame, embarrassed, or generally bad about what they have done. Therefore, lecturing them will not help the situation. Rather it will likely make them feel worse and then associate those negative feelings with you: a consequence that will be counterproductive to your goal of having them listen to you.

Rather than lecturing them, comfort them in their time of need and shame and help them to feel better. Then, if the behavior is repeatedly or hinted at being repeated, simply remind them of how it turned out and how it made them feel last time.

By being a guiding voice of support, rather than the nagging voice of a lecturer, your child is more likely to not only listen to you but respect your voice and opinion as well (Glembolk, 2014).

Say Thank You

Just as important and ensuring your tone of voice and tone of message in your request for proper behavior, it is also important to thank your child for their behavior.

If you word your request as a favor to you, then your child is more likely to listen. This is because if their behavior is a favor to you then you will be grateful for their actions, rather than simply feeling as though you are ordering them around. Therefore, if you thank them for their behavior, they are more likely to behave again, as they see that you are grateful for them behaving properly.

Be sure to thank them after they have performed the proper or requested action. However, it is also important to thank them before the action is completed and within the request itself; for example, "Can you please bring me the remote? Thank you," "Remember we sit on the couch, thank you," or "Please walk honey, thank you."

By including your gratitude within the question, in addition to thanking them after the behavior, you will ensure that your gratitude is known.

Focus on Comprehension

Another way that will make your child listen to you is to focus on compensation of the request. Many times that your child will not listen, and consequently behave poorly, is because they do not understand the request for behavior, or they do not understand why the behavior is not allowed.

For this reason, try to add a qualifying statement to your request that explains why the behavior or action is being asked for. An example of this would be, "Remember we walk in the house; if we run, we can get hurt," "Eat all of your vegetables please because that is how you grow big and strong," or even "Eat all of your vegetables please, then you can have some chocolate."

By adding in an explanatory phrase that explains your request, you will be helping them to understand why you are asking for specific behavior, in addition to not lecturing them.

Give Choices

A tricky and subtle way of making children listen to you is to make it seem as though they are not listening to you at all, but rather that they are making the rules. One nearly foolproof way of doing so is to give your child choices. This way, you are giving your child the feeling of power and control they crave while simultaneously receiving the proper behavior.

For example, if there are chores to be done, give your child a choice of three or four options of chores that they can do. The choices can be anything you choose them to be: dust, walk the dog, take out the trash, or do the dishes. Then, your child will then feel as though it is their choice to do that chore.

You can be rather cunning with the options you place in front of your child. For instance, you include the behavior or action that you want in the choices and pair it with chores or actions that you know your child will not choose.

No matter which options you give, and which option they choose, it is important to acknowledge how good their choice is. By saying "good choice" after your child makes the decision, it will justify the positive feelings they associate with the action in the future. Therefore, it makes it more likely for them to choose to act in such a way, or complete the task on their own without you giving them the option to.

Acknowledge Feelings

One reason that your children may not listen to you as it is their way of trying to show you how they feel.

For this reason, one way to encourage your child to listen to you is to acknowledge their feelings and emotions. Being a child can be stressful, as there are many instances of being unsure of yourself, not understanding what others are asking of you, and not knowing how to communicate your feelings.

Therefore, one way to help your children listen to you more is to get them to trust you; a way to get them to trust you is to acknowledge their feelings and help them come to the realization of their feelings.

This tactic also helps your child listen then you acknowledge their feelings in relation to a certain task or behavior. Saying things like, "I know you never like to brush your teeth because it makes your mouth feel funny, but how about we try a new toothpaste to see if it helps?" By validating their feelings, you are making your child feel respected in their opinion and are therefore more likely to respect you back and listen to your request.

When your child feels respected and allowed to have feelings toward certain requests, you will also lessen the chance of them having a tantrum or acting out as a response to an action or task that they do not want to do. Rather, the resistance you will be met with will likely be a calm response of how and why they dislike the request. Ultimately, you will open a dialogue and come to a compromise for the behavior (Finlay, 2020).

Allow Things to Happen

One of the more frustrating aspects of getting your child to listen to you is when they repeatedly do not listen, thereby making you feel forced to step in, be the bad guy, and stop them from doing something.

Therefore, you should try to simply let things happen. Allow for certain consequences to unfold if your child does not listen. Of course, excluding any consequences that are life threatening or severe, if you have repeatedly warned your child of consequences for their actions—or lack of actions—then allow these consequences to happen. Many individuals, adults and children alike, need to learn for themselves. Therefore, if you have told your child that if they continue a certain action there will be a certain consequence, then allow that consequence to happen.

By resolving that you will only ask or tell your child to do something a select number of times, then allow for the consequences to happen, you are avoiding the chance of nagging, in addition to allowing your child to learn on their own what the consequences are. Eventually, by experiencing that the consequences match up with what you have warned, your child will build trust in what you say, thereby lessening the chances of the failure to listen being due to mistrust.

Whisper

When you want someone to listen to you, generally or specifically, you have to draw their attention and focus to what you are saying. One way to do this is to lower the volume of your voice, or whisper, when you speak.

To be clear, it is still important for your voice to be clear and audible; whispering does not mean tricking your intended listener into thinking your message is unclear. Rather, the goal of whispering, or simply lowering your voice, is to make your intended listener work slightly harder, push away distractions, and focus on your voice and message. By naturally making your listener work slightly harder, you are making them focus on your message and increasing the chances of them understanding your message.

This technique works for children, as it counteracts the possible failure in listening of preoccupation. By lowering your voice, your child will need to push away any other preoccupations in their mind in order to listen to you. Even if they do not follow the direction, they are being forced to listen which increases the chance of them doing what you have asked.

One more benefit of whispering or lowering your voice is that you are going against what is expected and shocking—in a good way—your child into listening. If you or your child are used to a raised voice when being asked to do something, speaking quietly will shake up the norm and bring them into focus.

Turn Listening Into a Game

The last suggestion for how you can better your child listening skills is to help your children practice this skill. Of course, forcing your child to practice may have a counterproductive effect as they may feel as though they are in school again.

Children are meant to, and want to, have fun. For this reason, you should try and turn listening exercises into games. The proven and best way to teach your child how to develop a new skill is to teach them without their knowledge of what is going on, and sneak education and skill development into a game.

Do not get discouraged here thinking that we are leaving the development and creation of these games completely up to you. Following the conclusion of this book, there are a few help guides, one of which will be extremely helpful to you in the realm of listening games. Help Guide #2 includes a comprehensive list of common games—some of which your child may already be familiar with—that help you focus and hone your child's listening skills (McCreedy, n.d.).

Chapter 3:

How to Listen to Your Kids

Of course, perhaps the best way to help your child develop their listening skills, and in turn listen to you more effectively, is to project and embody the listening you want to see from them in yourself.

By showing them how you expect to be listened to, you are increasing your chances of improving your child's listening skills for a few different reasons. First, you are showing them that the expectations of listening are for everyone, not just them. Therefore, this makes them see that they are not being punished or left out for needing to learn how to listen.

Secondly, you are helping them to see how the different skills are used and applied to the listening process. Although there are many aspects of the listening process that adults and other experienced listeners take for granted, as they happen automatically and without thought, for the child who is just learning, some of the factors and aspects of proper listening can be challenging to understand. Therefore, by embodying the different aspects of active and proper listening, you are helping your child to understand how the process works.

A third benefit to embodying the listening you want from your child is that you are showing your child that you respect them and see them as an equal. Many problems that arise with your children not listening stem from the fact the child feels as though they are being talked down to and feel as though they are lesser than others or older children (WomensMedia, 2012).

How to Embody Active Listening

Active listening is a simple enough concept to grasp for adults. Generally speaking, it means to pay attention to the person who is speaking, or the sound and auditory stimuli in question, and respond in a way to show that you were paying attention, and you understand the meaning of what was being said.

There are some general ways to show active listening, in addition to certain gestures that can help you in specific situations to show understanding. The following is a list of some of the general ways to show active listening and some of the specific ways to show your child that you are actively listening to them.

Eye Contact

The first way to show your child that you are listening is to is to make eye contact with them. Just as talking with another adult, making eye contact with your child while they speak shows them that you are paying attention to them and that you want to hear what they have to say. While adults may understand that you can still be listening while doing other things, children have yet to develop this understanding. For this reason, it is important to show them, with our bodies, that we are listening to what they have to say.

Furthermore, children listen to our body language perhaps more than our words. Therefore, if they see that we are willing to stop what we are doing to listen to them, they will be more likely to speak to us. This may seem like a small aspect when it comes to improving the communication between you and your child; however, it has a much larger impact than you may think. After all, if your child sees that you are willing to show interest in what they are saying when the issue is small, they will feel confident and safe coming to you when the issue is larger and perhaps more difficult to talk about.

Making eye contact with them is one impactful way to show them that you are listening to them. Of course you do not have to drop everything to make eye contact. If you are doing something that requires your attention for safety purposes, such as making dinner, explain to your child that you will listen to them once you have a safe moment to do so; then, make sure you make the time to turn around away from the stove soon after to make eye contact and listen (CDC, 2019).

Be Relaxed

Again, children read our body language and tone perhaps more often and effectively than the words we use; this is especially true the younger the child is. This is because children are more emotional than logical. They also may have difficulty finding the right words or understanding some of the words and phrases you choose to communicate with. Therefore, it is important to communicate through our demeanor as well.

One demeanor that encourages and tells your child that you are listening is to be calm and relaxed. Even through times of stress and frustration, in general and with your child, it is important to remain relaxed and calm as you listen to what your child is saying. In doing so, you are showing that you are a safe person to come to when they need a person to talk to.

Also, it shows that you are mirroring the behavior you want to see from them in yourself. By staying calm and relaxed, even in times of listening to something you are not happy with, it will show the child that they are able to stay calm and relaxed even if you are asking them to do something they do not want to do (Bryant, n.d.).

Listen to the Words and Repeat What You Hear

Another way of showing that you are listening is to listen to the words that your child is saying and in the manner in which they are saying them.

This may seem like a no-brainer when it comes to listening, but you will be surprised how little listening people actually do. Especially when it comes to listening to children, we tend to try and listen for a whole message rather than listen to the works they are saying and discerning meaning from there.

When it comes to children, especially young children in the toddler range, they may have trouble forming full and complete sentences that hold one direct message. It also shows that the words they choose may be distorted or simply wrong for their message. Due to this, their message may not be coming across as they intended.

For this reason, it is important to listen to the words they say and repeat the words you hear clearly back to them. This way, they have a chance to listen to what they said and either confirm or deny the idea.

This way, you are also showing your child that it is okay to ask questions about what you hear so make sure that they understand.

Do Not Interrupt

Even though it is encouraged for you to repeat the words back to them, it is important that you resist the urge to interrupt. Additionally, sometimes what your child is saying can take a while to get out.

However, by interrupting them, you are showing your child that what they are saying is not as important as what you wish to say. You are also showing them that what you know is more important than whatever they are trying to tell you.

If interrupting your child's words is repeated, you are also allowing them to see that not letting someone else finish speaking is a regular and acceptable thing to do, thereby leading them to interrupt you when you speak.

It is important to remember that children do not understand the difference between you interrupting them for clarification and you butting in because you are not interested in what they are saying. To them, the message is conveyed that they too do not have to listen to your full sentence or idea when you speak.

Pay Attention and Show Interest

This suggestion has been alluded to throughout the above methods of listening, but it comes to its climax here. It is incredibly important that you show interest in what your child is saying and actually pay attention.

Again, this may seem like a natural part of listening, but you will be shocked to discover how little attention is being paid when anyone talks, let alone children.

One other way to show your interest and ensure that you are paying attention to what they say is to ask questions after your child is done speaking. The question can be anything that relates back to what they had just said. If they are asking for something, you can ask them to choose between a few choices of the object they want. If they are telling you a story, you may want to ask questions that encourage them to reflect on the story and provide more details. If your child is sharing with you a difficult emotion, you can ask supportive questions about how they wish you to help them or what will make them feel better.

By asking questions, you are showing that you not only paid attention to what they said but you are also interested in getting more details. There are also reverse benefits of showing interest in what your child says. If you do this often, your child will learn to reciprocate the behavior and are more likely to listen and pay attention when you speak (WomensMedia, 2020).

Know the Importance of Nonverbal Cues

Of course, and as stated above many times, speaking is hard, and when it comes to younger children, there may be cognitive issues that come along with a message not being communicated effectively. That does not mean that there is a cognitive learning disability that is preventing a message from coming through; rather, it simply means that your child may be too young to communicate what they mean clearly.

For this reason, it is important to pay attention to not only the words they say, but their nonverbal cues as well. Nonverbal cues are largely body language based. What are they doing while they are talking to you? What were they doing right before they began talking? What made them stop their action and turn to speak to you? Asking yourself these questions will help you to be able to discern what they mean.

Furthermore, by mentioning their body language in their response in either a neutral or positive way, you are helping your child to understand that how they use their body to communicate is important.

Do Not Judge

Not judging anyone is perhaps that most difficult part of listening, whether your counterpart is a child or an adult.

However, when it comes to not judging children, the task can be even more difficult, as there are two general ways that you can judge them. First, you can judge them for what they say as being a part of their personality. For example, if they are asking for a treat multiple times a day, you may judge your child as being spoiled or not understanding that healthy foods are a better choice. The other way in which judging can come in when listening to your children is that you can retroactively judge yourself. Again, if your child constantly asks for a treat, you may judge your own parenting style and question what you have done to make them think that treats are a regular snack, rather than the occasional foods.

No matter which way you judge, judging the situation will almost always yield negative effects because you will either gain a poor image or your child or of yourself. Both are not productive or useful images to have.

Therefore, it is important to keep your reactions and judgements positive or neutral when it comes to bad behaviors. If your child feels as though you view them and judge them for their actions, they are less likely to come to you with larger issues later on in their life (CDC, 2019).

Get Rid of Distractions

Another way of showing your child that you are listening is to actively push away any distractions that may hinder your understanding of what is being said. Of course, this does not mean to drop everything the moment your child begins talking.

Rather, take a moment to push away the distractions, and step away from what you were doing before you turn to listen. By taking those moments to ensure that you are safely and confidently stepping away from your distractions, it will lessen the chances of you feeling rushed to get back to it in time. For example, if you are cooking dinner, be sure to lower the temperature, wash your hands, or put the knife down in a safe place so you feel as though you can give your child your full attention. Even if your distraction seems subtle such as watching TV, be sure to mute the show or pause your movie so you are not making your child's voice compete with the sounds of the television.

Again, your child can read your mood better than you think they can. If they feel as though you are rushing to get back to what you were doing, or if you do not take the time to turn away from what you are doing, then your child may feel guilty or bad for wanting to talk to you; even worse, they may feel as though they are not as important as your task.

Furthermore, you are showing your child that it is okay to be distracted by something else when another person is trying to talk to you.

* * *

Of course, embodying the different aspects of active listening can be difficult to do as it involves you putting your ego or importance aside and turning your focus onto your child and what they are trying to communicate with you.

However, try to remember that there is a mutual win when it comes to listening to your child. First, you are gaining information about how your child talks, speaks, and communicates. This knowledge is truly invaluable, as it will help you get to know your child more as a person. Secondly, you are showing them how you wish them to listen to you and allowing them to see and develop proper listening skills.

However, this win-win is really a threefold win and benefit, as you will also be encouraging your child to open up to you more and bring you closer as a parent and child. By listening to your child actively and showing them that you respect them, you are also showing them that they can come to you with any future problem without the fear of judgement or being reprimanded (Bryant, n.d.).

Part 2:

Communication

Chapter 4:

Why Communication Fails

To understand how communication fails, you must first understand how communication works.

Interestingly, the mechanisms of communication are easy concepts to understand, either as whole or through its parts. That being said, it is a difficult process to put into practice, as it can fail or be compromised in some way.

Generally, communication is conceptually broken down into four parts: the sender, the message, the channel, and the receiver (Communication Theory, 2014):

Sender

The first part and step to communication is the sender. This is the person, or people, that are intending to send and share their message with other people or another person.

The sender can and will change throughout the entirety of a conversation. It is the responsibility of the sender to ensure that their message is as clear as they can make it. However, no matter how clear they believe their message to be, there are three more steps and parts of communication through which their message can be skewed.

Message

The message itself is the next important aspect of communication. The message itself must be one that holds a clear intention and meaning. In order for the communication to be successful, there must be a clear meaning to the message.

If you think back to when you have been successful and unsuccessful in your communication, you will probably notice a trend that when your message is simple and clear, it is better received, and your communication is more successful.

For this reason, the message itself, how it is constructed, and what it is intending to communicate also plays a factor into how successful the communication is.

Channel

The third aspect important to communication is the channel. The channel of a message is how the message is delivered and sent from the first person, and how it is received by the second person.

The channel of the message can be different in its specifics, yet generally the channel of the message can be placed in one of three categories: verbal, written, or nonverbal. These channel categories and classifications will be differentiated further in this chapter.

Receiver

The last piece that is needed for communication to be successful is the receiver. The receiver is meant to be the person, or people, that the message is aimed at. In order for the communication to be successful, the receiver must be able to receive the message, decode the meaning of the message, and accept the meaning into their faculties of understanding. As we explored in the listening chapter, the receiver must go through the different steps of listening in order for the communication to be successful.

* * *

All four of these aspects and parts of communication have to be present in order for the communication to have a hope of being successful. Often, these different parts of communication are taken for granted as many of us think communication is a linear process from one person's mouth to another person's ear. In fact, these four above parts of the communication process are not the only participants that play a role in whether or not communication fails. Other aspects to consider when analyzing communication are the specifications of the channel, the details of the message, the message, and the conversation type or context.

Specifications of the Channel

As mentioned above, there are three different specifications or classifications of the channel that the message can fall into. The first is oral or verbal communication. This is communication that comes from the mouth of one person, and it is audible to other people and the receiver. Generally, verbal communication is talking; however, it can also be lecturing, shouting, protesting, or crying.

To directly contrast verbal communication, the second channel type is nonverbal communication. This is any communication that does not create a sound or audible sense when it is created and sent to the intended receiver. Formal and practiced sign language is one pinnacle example of nonverbal communication; however, perhaps a lesser known or considered example could also be generalized body language, facial expressions, and eye contact. Almost all of us have been able to discern meaning from the body language of another individual.

The third and final channel of communication is written communication. Although this is technically classified as nonverbal communication, written communication deserves its own category because there is so much involved in it. Written communication can be anything from a picture to a text message to a street sign, making it one of the more diverse types and channels of communication.

In order for communication to be successful, the channel of communication must be understood and accepted by both the sender and the receiver.

Details of the Message

The details of the message refer to what the meaning and content of the message is. This is an important aspect of whether or not the communication is successful because not only does the sender have to ensure that their intended meaning comes through in the detail of their message, but they must also ensure that the message is one that the receiver can understand and accept.

On the other hand, there is also the responsibility of the receiver to ensure that they are getting and understanding the full extent of the message. It is their responsibility to ask for clarification if certain details come across as unclear or muddled.

Many individuals believe that it is the opposing person's responsibility to ensure the clarity of the details are present. This is true no matter the position or role in the communication. However, both the sender and the receiver have their own part of the message that they are responsible for (EDUCBA, 2020).

Conversation Type

There are two types of conversation: formal and informal. Formal conversations are those situations that require or ask for a certain level of respect, education, and etiquette from all participants. Alternatively, there is informal communication, which are situations that are more relaxed and can handle a certain amount of casualty and familiarity that would otherwise be deemed inappropriate.

To go through the different types of communication and their specific situations would be a lengthy process; however, the distinction can be one that is intuitive to most people. To make the distinction, think about when you have made yourself reflect on what you were about to say, practice your message and meaning, or think of when you were nervous for the success of the communication. More often than not, these are instances of formal conversations.

On the other hand, if you find yourself swearing, using slang or colloquial phrases, or if you find the conversation flows more easily without worry, then you are most likely in an informal instance of communication (EDUCBA, 2020).

Why Does Communication Fail?

Based on all of the different factors that go into communication, it is clear that there are many different options and ways in which communication can fail. For instance, if any of the above factors fails to be adhered to or exercised properly, then the communication fails. Allow us to give some examples.

First, if you are in a formal situation and conversation, and you begin to act in a way that is perhaps too informal, then your partners in conversation may not accept or listen to what you are trying to share. This is because in a formal setting, informality is often considered as inappropriate and that you are not educated or polite enough to conform to the formalities. On the other hand, if you act too formal in an informal conversation, you can come across as pompous and condescending, thereby encouraging someone else to not listen or accept what you are sharing.

Another example is if the channel does not transfer from the sender to the receiver, then the communication will fail as well. For example, if you are using sign language to someone who does not understand this nonverbal form of communication, then of course your communication will not be successful. Alternatively, if you write a message for an individual who cannot read, or who does not understand the written communication, then your message and meaning will not get through.

One last example of how communication fails using the parts of communication described above is that the details of the message do not come across as they were intended. Meaning, emotions, and ideas are all complicated concepts to communicate. It is rare that you will find the exact words that translate to an exact meaning, message, or idea that you wish to communicate. For this reason, the sender has the responsibility to combine the different signs, symbols, and words to present their message as intended. Of course, there can be some discrepancy in what a word or a sign means to the sender and what that same word or sign means to the receiver. Therefore, the message can be skewed and manipulated, again ultimately leading to a fail in communication.

Of course, although there are possible communication fails based on each of the communication parts and factors mentioned above, there are also generalized communication failures that have to do with external aspects of the conversation itself.

There Are Too Many Senders

In order for communication to work, one message must transfer from the sender through the channel into the receiver before another sender sends another message. Otherwise, if too many senders are sharing their message at once, rather than waiting for the receiver to accept the message, then messages can become mixed together, convoluted, and confusing.

Take for example a group outing where multiple people are talking at once. It is difficult to discern between what is being said and the message is being shared. Furthermore, it is nearly impossible to be productive in moving forward in the conversation if too many individuals are talking at once. This is because no one is acting as the receiver; no one is listening to what is being said. Instead, messages are being sent out to fall on theoretically deaf ears (Wrike, n.d.).

To possibly rectify the conversational failure of too many senders, take a moment to step back and be the receiver. Take a moment to not send a message, and try to accept and understand some of the messages that are being sent out.

No Trust or Respect

Another reason that conversation and communication may fail is that there is no trust or respect within the relationship. The sender must respect the person and group of individuals they are communicating with so as to ensure that their message is respectful itself. Individuals are more likely to listen, understand, and accept a message when it is presented in a respectful way. Moreover, the sender must trust that the receiver will do their part in the communication process. That is to say that the sender must trust that the receiver will ask for clarification in the message if needed, critically analyze the message and information, and use the information properly.

Conversely, the receiver must also trust and respect the sender. If the receiver holds no respect for the other individual who is sharing a message with them, then they are more likely to disregard the information or simply not to listen. Once more, it is important for the receiver to trust that the sender is presenting their message as clearly and as effectively as possible. Also, if there is some sort of confusion within the message, the receiver must trust that the message was not purposefully manipulated so as to confuse them. After all, if the receiver feels deliberately manipulated or deceived, they are less likely to ask for clarification of the message (Wrike, n.d.).

Assuming Knowledge

Another reason as to why communication would fail, that is influenced by external factors and not necessarily buy the parts of the conversation themselves, is that there could be an incorrectly assumed amount of knowledge on the part of either the sender or the receiver.

Where communication fails in this sense is when the sender assumes a certain level or kind of knowledge held by the receiver, when in reality the receiver is not at the assumed level. This does not mean that the receiver is not as intelligent as the sender assumed they would be. It can simply be that the receiver is not as knowledgeable in a specified area or that the receiver does not have a full grasp of a specific language that the sender is using.

The problem with assuming a certain knowledge type of your receiver is that your message may not be as clear as it should be in order to make sure that your message and meaning is getting across effectively.

Interestingly, and important to note here, is that it is not always the case that the sender assumes a higher level of knowledge than the receiver has. In fact, it is common for the sender to assume that the receiver has a lower level of knowledge. As a result, the sender may oversimplify their message, thereby leading to their message and communication coming off as patronizing and condescending (Paramapoonya, 2017).

Failure to Listen

Perhaps the easiest explanation as to why communication fails is because the other individual is simply not listening. As discussed in the previous section, there is a difference between hearing and listening.

Of course, there are many different reasons that go into why communication fails. However, and unfortunately, most times the communication fails simply because the receiver, or the person intended to be the receiver, is simply not listening (Johansson, 2016).

* * *

Of course when it comes to communication, and their respective failures of communication, often it is discussed within the scope of a business or an office setting.

However, the same reasoning, justification, and philosophy can be applied to communication breakdowns and failures between a parent and their children. For example, parents often will assume that their child knows and understands the expectations of the parent and their meaning when they communicate; however, this is not always the case. Furthermore, the child may be experiencing a failure to listen properly, therefore not fully accepting the message from their parent. Lastly, there may simply be too many senders at once. In an attempt to get their message across, the parent may not allow time for their child to respond. Alternatively, in an attempt to take the power from their parents, the child may be interrupting the parent when they speak.

Specific ways in activities of avoiding and mending the different failures in conversation between a parent and their child will be discussed in the following two chapters.

Chapter 5:

How to Talk to Your Kids

As discussed above, there are two roles or positions that an individual can play in an instance of communication or in a communicative relationship. Namely, they are the sender or the receiver. In order to improve your communication with your child, you must ensure that you are being the most effective sender and receiver (Child Development, 2019).

This chapter specifically focuses on improving your communication skills as a sender of the message.

Use Their Name

The suggestion when talking to your child is to use their name. When you use anyone's name when you speak with them, you are doing a few different things that increase the level of conversation.

First, you are making sure that they know you are talking with them, as you verbally direct the conversation toward them. When someone uses your name, it is harder to ignore them or have selective hearing. Secondly, you are bringing a level of intimacy to the conversation that would otherwise be lacking. When it comes to speaking with your children, this intimacy is more akin to a kind of closeness or connectedness that you create with your child. Third, you are validating the other person's identity when you use their name. The name of a person is the first way they and others identify them. Therefore, when you use their name, and use their name properly, you are validating their identity within the conversation.

Of course, this does not mean that you have to repeat their name at the beginning, middle, and end of every sentence within the conversation.

However, even simply putting it within one sentence is enough to bring their attention to you and for you to show your respect toward them.

Positive Language

Another way to have effective conversation and communication with your child is to use positive language. As mentioned above in the chapters about listening, using negative words such as "no" or "don't" can yield undesired consequences.

Think back to when you last heard the word "no" from a friend, coworker, or other person you deem equal or to have more authority than you. You most likely felt defeated and let down by their answer. Furthermore, if you reflect on those instances where someone has repeatedly said "no" to you, you probably do not look favorably on them. Even if you think back to how you feel when your child says "no" to you, you will find similar emotions within yourself.

The same negative thoughts and emotions are experienced by your child when you overuse these negative words as well. In fact they may even be more likely to not listen to you if you are continuously negative. For this reason, in order to have productive communication with your child, try to keep the message positive.

Of course, this does not mean that you cannot discipline or be stern with your child, nor does this mean that you can never use negative language. Rather, by reworking your phrase and message to have a positive tone, and only using the negative words sporadically, you can strengthen the effectiveness of your communication and increase the impact when you do use negative words.

Connect With Them

Another way to make your communication with your child more effective is to connect with them. Connection in this sense does not mean that you have to speak like a teenager or child, nor does it mean you have to use their slang or pop culture references in order to get your message across. Instead, this means to physically connect with your child when you speak to them.

Just as removing distractions and looking your child in the eye while they speak to you is important, doing the same when you speak to them reciprocates the respect and shows them that you are trying to connect with them.

Another way of creating this connection is to include a physical touch in the interaction. Instances of physical touching can help to bridge the gap between sending a message and having the other person receive the message clearly. For example, if you want to show your child that you empathize with them, you may want to give them a hug or a gentle back rub. This small physical gesture, even if you intend on being stern with them, shows them that you at least empathize with their struggle, though they will think there is a lesson to be learned.

Use Volume to Your Advantage

Another suggestion to make your communication more effective with your child is to play with and use volume to your advantage. Using the same example as above, whispering can help you draw your child's attention to what you say as they naturally pay closer attention to your words in order to hear you, let alone actually listen to what you are saying.

However, lowering the volume is not the only way you can use volume to your advantage. Speaking in a clear and level toned voice and volume can help to convey the message that what you are saying is of importance and that you are intending for others to hear clearly what you are saying.

Furthermore, speaking calmly and at a level that is natural for people to speak at can help to convey a meaning of respect and equal comradery between you and your child, so as to drive home the notion that they are worthy conversational partners.

Keep It Simple

One reason as to why communication may fail, as mentioned above, is because the message is unclear. Therefore, it is important to keep your message as simple as possible when communicating with others.

That being said, keeping a message simple does not mean to dumb down the message. In fact, "simplifying" the message in this way can come off as patronizing and condescending, therein leading to your receiver not listening to your message at all.

To ensure that you are simplifying your message while not dumbing it down too much, think about the general and overall message that you wish to convey and break that down into different talking points. By making different aspects of your overall meaning into different talking points where you give the other person a chance to respond, you are making it seem as though they are coming to the meaning of the conversation together with you, as opposed to you lecturing to your partner.

Making sure that your message is simple and clear, but you are not being patronizing in your presentation, is a fine line that is important when talking to your children. However, with practice and an open line of communication with your child, the line can be walked with great success.

Ask Them to Repeat

Asking your child to repeat what they have said is another indirect way of improving your communication with them.

First, asking them to repeat themselves shows them that you are interested in what they are saying and that you either want to know more, or are interested in having them clarify when they have said, depending on the conversation. In the end, this shows them that you also respect what they are saying so much that you trust them to elaborate.

Secondly, by asking your child to repeat themselves, you are showing them a sense of humility in your conversation and embodying the fact that asking for clarification, or admitting that you do not know something in a conversation, is okay. Many children, or the individuals in general for that matter, feel a sense of anxiety or embarrassment when they do not understand the message that is being communicated with them. Therefore, if you ask them to clarify what they mean, you are showing them that even you as an authority figure are humble enough to ask for clarification.

As a third benefit to a suggestion, by asking your child to repeat themselves, you are also telling them that a specific point or message in what they said is unclear. Therefore, they will, either consciously or subconsciously, remember how to better express themselves in the future if they want to get that message across.

Ultimately, you are allowing your child to develop a strong sense of self and identity in their conversations, in addition to allowing them to understand the best way of communicating certain messages.

Legs First, Mouth Second

One last suggestion that can help you to improve the overall level of conversation between you and your child is to follow the philosophy of legs first and mouth second. This philosophy claims that conversation is more effective when the individuals make the effort to physically be close to one another.

For example, if you were to talk to a colleague within your workplace, you would not call them from another room, or office. Furthermore, you would not shout it to them from far away and assume that they heard you properly. Rather, in order to ensure that your message is received, you will walk over to that person—whether they be in a different office or room—and then share your message with them. In doing so, you are not only lessening the chances of your message not being received, but you are also showing your conversational partner that you respect them.

The same philosophy should be adopted when speaking to your children. Try to avoid shouting to your child from another room, or speaking to them from far away. Instead, walk into the room before asking your child to do whatever you wish. This way, your child will feel as though they cannot ignore your request as they are right in front of you, in addition to feeling respected as you cared enough to come into the room to speak to them.

* * *

Ultimately, your child wants to feel as though they are respected and loved by you. Of course, you can show them through telling them you love them and your actions; however, it is in the smaller instances of communication where the most meaning is transmitted.

Therefore, if you focus on respect, even when being stern or disciplining your child, you can still speak to them in a way that shows you respect them yet you are the boss. In fact, they are more likely to listen to you and see you as an authority figure and role model if you speak to them with respect (Child Development, 2019).

Interestingly, these same suggestions on how to speak and communicate better with your children are the same suggestions that can help improve your conversations with adults and other people as well. This goes to show that the key to speaking effectively with people is to keep the same level of respect in every conversation you have.

Chapter 6:

How to Get Your Kids to Talk to

You

To continue and round out the section on communication, it is now time to practice your skills as a receiver of messages within the communication structure. Indeed, it is difficult to understand, and even wrap your head around, the fact that in order for the communication between you and your child to be effective, you must give them the option and opportunity to be the sender.

After all, by embodying the pinnacle and ideal archetype of what a receiver in the structure and relationship of communication should be, you are giving an example to your children of what you expect of them when you are the sender and they are the receiver. The key to a more effective and less problematic communicative relationship between you and your child, especially with younger children who are learning and developing the skills, is to show your child your expectations through your actions, not just telling them the expectations through your words.

Ultimately, by showing that you are a good receiver, you will in turn allow and encourage your children to talk to you and communicate with you more.

Why Won't Your Child Talk to You?

Although there are many reasons as to why your children may not feel as though they can or want to talk to you, the following are the most common and likely reasons why you may find your children are closed off to you in the conversational department (Schwarz, 2017):

Solve Their Problems

The first reason as to why your children may not talk to you is because you solve their problems. When your child is young and as they develop, their initial instinct is to look to you to satisfy any needs or answer any questions they may have.

However, if you are consistently anticipating their needs, thereby removing the requirement of them to physically ask you for something, then your child may develop a belief that they do not have to speak to you. The other issue is that they will believe that you will always be there to anticipate their needs, therein never requiring them to verbalize what they want. Believing that you will always anticipate their needs can lead your child to be short-tempered at times because if you do not anticipate their needs correctly, they do not have the ability to verbalize or communicate what they actually wanted.

You Talk Too Much

Similarly, another reason as to why your child may not speak to or communicate with you as much as you would like is because you yourself talk too much. When your child is learning how to communicate, they need more time to develop their meaning and message before they verbalize it. This means that not only do you have to be patient in expecting your child to answer a question, you must give them enough time and enough silence in order for them to have the confidence to answer.

Think about when you are in a large group of people, and there are many individuals talking. People who have a lower sense of self-confidence are likely to stay quiet and not speak up or talk at all. This is because they do not feel as though there is enough time for them to communicate their message effectively.

The same philosophy can be applied to your child. This does not mean that your child has a low sense of self-confidence. Rather, it means that in those years where they are developing their sense of self-esteem and self-confidence, it is important to ensure that they feel as though they are able to communicate with you.

You Are Judgmental

Being judgmental of what your child says is another reason as to why your child may not be communicating with you as much as you would like. In general, a child does not like to talk with or communicate with someone who is negatively judging every message they try to send.

If the child feels as though you are going to negatively judge what they will say, then they may feel as though they do not want to talk to you. Being judgmental can be communicated in criticizing or asking condescending questions after every message.

Even if you do not agree with the opinion, or the message of what your child is trying to say, it is important to keep your opinion as judgmental free as possible. Of course, there are ways to share a counter opinion without being condescending or judgmental. For example, rather than asking questions that criticized what your child has said or asked of you, try asking questions that clarify their opinion or ask for them to further explain. In doing so, you will not only learn perhaps their reasoning toward their opinion, which may lessen your negative judgment toward them, but you can help them come to a different opinion altogether.

You Are Distracted

A fourth reason as to why your child may not talk to you or communicate with you as openly as you wish is because you are constantly distracted. In the chapters above, we talked about the importance of limiting distractions when you listen and talk to your child. Generally, removing distractions when your child is talking to you, and when you are talking to your child, shows that you respect them and are ready to receive their message, whatever it may be.

However, if you tend to multitask when your child talks, or refuse to look up from a screen or from your work, your child may feel as though you not only are not interested in what they have to say, but you do not respect them as a communicator, either.

Therefore, not only is removing distractions an imperative step to helping your child learn how to listen better, it is also an important aspect to encouraging your child to communicate more openly and consistently with you.

You Pressure Them

Explanation as to why your child may be closed off to you is because you pressure them to open up. The only thing that shines under pressure are diamonds; most other objects and people crumble and break down once they are under immense amounts of pressure.

When your child is learning how to communicate, it is important for them to come up with and develop the meaning and message that they want to send on their own. If you force them to communicate when they have no message to send, then they may become confused as to the purpose of communication in the first place.

Also, the more that you pressure them into communicating when they do not want to, your child may eventually develop a poor or anxiety-based relationship with communication. Ultimately, this anxiety-based relationship can lead to more serious anxiety disorders, depression, allow others to talk for them, and a general inability to communicate with others.

How Can You Improve Their Communication?

If one or more of the above scenarios resonates with you, do not fret. Many parents find themselves in similar, if not the same, situations with their own children. To you and them, not all hope is lost. No matter the reasons that you think your child is closed off to you, there are ways to rectify and improve the communication between you two (Sears, 2020):

Never Give Unsolicited Advice

If you believe the reasons your children do not open up to you is because you talk too much or solve their problems, one way to rectify this is to not give unsolicited advice.

Parents, through no fault of their own, like to show their children that they are a figure of authority by spouting and sharing an endless stream of life advice and suggestions on how their children should act.

However, in doing so, you are not allowing your child to come to you with specific problems or looking for specific advice.

Therefore, to encourage your children to come to you in search of help, hold off on stating your opinion or giving unsolicited advice. This will also reinforce the power and influence of the advice when you give it, as your child will not have heard the line many times before.

Let Them Fail

Again, to directly counteract the reason for you solving your child's problems, let them fail. As their parent, you have been placed in the position as helper, role model, guru, problem solver, and all-around guidance system for your children.

No matter the title you like the best, there is a pull for you to anticipate the needs of your child and stop them from doing anything bad or wrong. However, just as allowing the consequences to unfold when you are teaching your child to listen, the same approach can be used when you are encouraging your child to open up to you.

By letting them fail, you are giving them the opportunity to come to you with a problem for you to solve, rather than having you solve problems before they even happen. Moreover, by allowing them to fail in certain cases, you are encouraging them to develop their own problem-solving skills to solve their own problems. Many parents fear, at this point, that if their child solves their own problems, they will no longer have a need for their parents. This is not necessarily true. As solving their own problems will give your child a sense of pride, they will also want to share the good news with you that they were able to solve their own problems.

In turn, and indirectly to, allowing them to open up to you a little bit more.

Ask Open-Ended Questions

One way to encourage your children to talk to you more stems from a conversational philosophy for individuals who want to improve their overall conversational skills.

That is to ask open-ended questions. Open-ended questions are those questions that have more than one answer to them; these are also the questions that ask more of the person than to simply answer "yes" or "no."

Open-ended questions give the opportunity for there to be a conversation to be started and sustained between two or more people. These types of questions show their usefulness when encouraging your child to speak, as it allows your child to think of their answer rather than simply give one-word answers. Also, their answer can also give you ideas for follow-up questions to ask or make a comment on to further the conversation. If you make a routine of it, your child will begin to prepare their answers ahead of time and in turn learn to ask questions.

Eventually, the more you practice, your child will learn to open up to you without you having to ask the open-ended questions each day.

Find the in Between

Another way of mending the communicative relationship, one that directly tackles the chance of them feeling pressured to talk, is to find those in-between moments where talking comes naturally, and take advantage of those. For example, in-between times would be them walking home from the bus stop with you, or when they are putting on their pajamas for bed. Generally, they are times when talking is not the focus of the situation, and there are some intuitive questions and answers held within these times.

If during these times you ask small and point focused questions, ones that have simple answers, you will find that your child is more comfortable talking and answering you. You can ask them which pajamas they want to wear for bed, you can ask them specific questions about their school day on your walk home, or you can even ask them what they want to drink for dinner.

These easy questions during the in-between times will allow your child to become more comfortable with answering simple questions. Eventually, you can open up the questions to those times where talking is more of a focus—like during dinner time—and asking questions where you child has to think more about their answer. In doing so, and ensuring that your child knows that you are there to listen to them, you will help to develop your child's confidence in talking.

Treat Them Like a Person

If you have yet to find a thread of consistency throughout the suggestions of getting your child to listen and talk to you, one common suggestion is that you should treat them like another person.

If you talk or treat your child like a child, then they are more likely to behave as a child. As such, they will likely not develop communication skills in the way you would like. Instead, try to treat your child like another person: with respect and not in a patronizing way.

To be clear, this does not mean to talk to them about war, the stock market, or other age inappropriate topics. Instead, it means to simply treat them with respect and as a person who communicates their own ideas. As such, you will allow your child to understand that because you view them as an equal, they should feel comfortable going to you with any problem or topics to be discussed.

Talk to Them

One last suggestion to help improve your communicative relationship with your child is to talk to them. Many parents confuse talking to their children with answering their questions or telling them what to do. However, actual talking is so much more.

Your child takes the majority of their social and communication cues from you; therefore, if they only see you communicating with them when you want them to do something, they will mirror that behavior.

Talk to your kids. Talk to them about your day, talk to them about what you are thinking of having for dinner, or even talk to them about what your favorite movies are. Simply talk to them. The more diverse topics you talk about with your child, the more likely they are to understand that they can talk about a wide variety of topics with you.

Just be sure that you give them time to add to the conversations, and you make sure the topics and language are age appropriate, of course.

* * *

Ultimately, your child wants to know that you are a safe and open receiver to any message they wish to send. Also, the more you open yourself up to your child and how you communicate with them, the more likely they are to reciprocate and mirror those actions back to you.

Of course, many parents fear that opening a line of communication between themselves and their child may have a negative effect, as they feel as though an open line of communication leads to a lack of discipline or respect between child and parent, or that it may lead to needy and codependent children. Many studies have been done to show that having an open line of communication does not lead to poor discipline or children who take advantage of their parents. Rather, open and healthy lines of communication between parent and child lead to children who are stronger, have better social development, are sure of themselves, have a higher ability of communication, and have a higher sense of emotional intelligence.

Part 3:

Understanding

Chapter 7:

The Life of Your Child

Other than understanding how to be a better listener for your child and how to communicate better with your child, it is important to understand, or at least try to understand, the life of your child if you wish to form a stronger relationship with them.

For many parents, the animosity and conflict between parent and child comes from the fact that the parent does not understand why the child is acting in such a way, nor do they understand their child's reactions to certain things. In desperation, many parents throw their hands up in the air and ask, "Why can't my child just listen to me?" or "Why doesn't my child react the way that I want them to?"

In these instances, the parent is discounting the life of the child by itself. There is an assumption that the life of a child is one that is easy. For instance, your meals are made and prepared for you, you do not have to worry about what to wear throughout the day, you do not have to pay bills, you do not have to go to work, and you do not have the responsibilities of an adult.

Although this may be true, this does not mean that the life of the child is easy or that it does not contain stress. In fact, a child lives every day with a large amount of stress, as each day they are forced to learn and communicate in ways that they perhaps are not comfortable with, do not fully understand, or that are confusing to them. For instance, a younger toddler may throw a temper tantrum when out in public because they may have lost sight of their mother at one point and has become overwhelmed with a sea of unfamiliar faces. However, to the outside world, it would seem that the child is acting out for no apparent reason. Alternatively, for the older child, their life is no easier. They have to balance going to school and learning subjects that they may not understand, in addition to learning how to be okay and confident in their own skin and potentially experiencing different social injustice or bullying.

While the difference stresses that a child faces can seem to be smaller and less important than the stresses of an adult, it is important to recognize that to your child, these struggles and stresses that come off as minor inconveniences to adults, uproot their understanding of the world and are quite literally seen as worst-case scenarios and stresses (Lee, 2020).

When adults are stressed, and overly so, it is because they have found an obstacle that dramatically affects one or more areas of their life. The same thing happens to children who are stressed—they have been faced with a challenge and struggle that is negatively affecting one or more aspects of their lives.

The following is a list of possible pressures and stresses that a child can face over their lives.

School

There are many different stresses and pressures that come along with going to school. There are the pressures of fitting in with different cliques or groups of friends. There are the stresses of doing well in different subjects and making sure that they bring home a good report card. There are even stresses related to making sure that they finish assignments on time or even catch the bus on time.

All of these smaller instances of being stressed come together to create a larger, more influential trigger of stress for your child. Your calming and useful power as a parent can only reach so far. It does not take long for your child to realize that they are, technically, alone at school and are responsible for their own behavior. At home, they are safe and always have someone on their side who will support them, namely their parents. However, at school, it is different. There are different stresses and pressures that make them feel isolated and anxious.

What makes these stresses worse is what the homelife of the child adds to them. For example, if the parents are extremely forceful and strict in the grades that the child gets, this can cause stress.

As adults, we have a job that we attend every day and have different responsibilities and duties to complete each day. For children, their job, or one of their jobs, is school. Therefore, if you consider a child's school akin to an adult's job, it is easy to understand how a child can become overwhelmed by the pressures and stresses associated with it (Medline, n.d.).

Friends

The next general stress that your children may have to face is the stress of having friends. For the first few years of their lives, the only people that they interacted with were family or other children that they were brought to play with.

However, as your child grows and develops, it becomes their own responsibility to develop, nurture, and maintain their own friendships. It also becomes their responsibility to remove themselves from unhealthy friendships and relationships, whether they want to or not.

Additionally, there are a few smaller and multiple associated stresses that come with friendships. These would be the pressures of fitting in, the pressures of following what your friends are doing, and the pressures of feeling like you do not have enough friends or not the right friends.

Of course, in retrospect, making friends as a child is easy, especially when you consider it from the viewpoint of an adult. However, when you are a child and you are in the thick of it trying to formulate friendships, it can be a stressful and world-altering experience.

Balance

As adults, we are encouraged to find a balance between our work life, our personal life, and our school life. As children, there is a similar trio of factors to balance. They have to balance their homelife, their school life, and their own personal life.

Therefore, just as many adults find it hard to balance their own three important areas of their life, children find it just as difficult.

Perhaps children find it more difficult as they are less knowledgeable about the world and are able to make less decisions about their lives.

Not Living Their Own Life

Another stress that can be heavily burdening your child is the fact that they do not live their own lives. Of course, many children are very fortunate, and this is not a comment on the lives that you have built for your children. It is, however, a reference made to the fact that many of the decisions made throughout the day that regard your child are not made by themselves. Rather, most every decision is made by their parents or by another adult. As children grow, they get more and more responsibility, and they get to make more decisions about their day-to-day lives. However, for many children it is not until they leave home for the first time when they are in early adulthood that they actually begin to make true decisions about their own life.

This stress of having other people dictate the majority of your life can be stressful because children are being faced with conflicting messages. They are being told to be independent and take responsibility for their actions, all the while their parents are still making the majority of the decisions for them.

Again, this is not mentioned to suggest that you give your child more responsibility, nor is it mentioned to encourage you to allow your child to make decisions that they are simply not prepared for. It is simply meant to make you aware of the fact that this is another stress that is present in your child's everyday life.

Not Knowing Anything

Let us not forget that children genuinely enter the world not knowing anything. Then, as the years go on they are slowly introduced to the expanding world around them. This is a terrifying way of living if you think about it. Many adults take advantage of the fact that we have a general or working knowledge of how the days are structured, how people are generally going to act toward you, and have a set of expectations for the way the world works. Children do not have this luxury. Everything they encounter for the first half of their life is going to be new things and experiences.

Therefore, your child is also carrying with them an incredible stress of the unknown. Although it would seem that your child has taken to a daily routine relatively well, we must understand that the majority of their behavior is undertaken simply out of repetition, not through understanding their overall actions (Medline, n.d.).

Other Stresses

In addition to these stresses, there are other stresses and struggles that children are faced with in their lives that prove to stay with them throughout their lives.

For example, children also face issues and stresses related to:

- Developing self-esteem

- Feeling adequate

- Struggles with communicating difficult feelings and emotions

- Living up to expectations

- Trying to balance what they want with that they need and is good for them

- Peer pressure

- The ever-changing decline of our world and environment

- Learning life lessons, such as understanding love, loss, and disappointment

- Their health

* * *

Of course, you can acknowledge that your child is stressed all you want to. However, what is most important is for you to be able to recognize the different signs of stress in children in order to be able to help them through the different stresses.

The difference symptoms of stress found in children are similar to those found in adults; however, they have some subtle yet important differences. That is to say that stress manifests itself in some similar ways in children as in adults. For example, the child may have difficulty concentrating, may be more aggressive or short-tempered with other children, they may be clingy or codependent to other individuals that they trust, and they may exhibit physical symptoms of stress like headaches, nausea, and stomach aches (Lee, 2020).

Of course, the differences between adults and children are in the following symptoms of stress. These are perhaps more extreme symptoms of stress, but they are also the telltale signs that there is something within your child that is uneasy.

For instance, the child may begin to wet their bed, even if they were previously fully potty trained. The child may refuse to go to school if their stresses are concentrated in the academic area. They are not interested in their friends' favorite toys. They may develop a nervous habit or tick like biting their nails, chewing their hair, or even more seriously, practicing self-harm like scratching or cutting themselves.

Just as it is important to watch for signs of immense stress in adults, if any of these symptoms have emerged recently and suddenly without any known cause, then you should consult with your family doctor or physician to ensure that the stress does not escalate or compound into something more serious and dangerous. When it comes to children and stress, you can never be too safe. While you want them to experience certain stresses and challenges to help them grow and develop strong stress-relieving techniques, you do not want them to develop anxiety or other stress-related disorders or illnesses. For that reason, it would be smart, and is actively suggested and encouraged, that you keep an open line of communication between you and your child and you and your family doctor.

* * *

All of this is to say that the life of your child may not be as carefree or as simple as it may seem. Of course, this is not your fault; as a parent, it is nearly impossible to remove every stressor from a child's life. In fact, it is the stressors that help to develop strong, independent, and well-rounded adults. All you can do is help guide them through the different stresses, and help them to develop strong coping mechanisms to stress.

A few ways that you can help guide your child through the struggles, and prepare them for the harder struggle ahead, is to help them develop their communication skills and to listen to them when they need someone to talk to. Therefore, understanding that your child's life is in fact stressful, perhaps not to you but to them, will help you better connect with your child and develop a stronger bond with them. They will recognize that you respect and acknowledge their stresses, and will in turn show their appreciation by respecting and acknowledging you.

Chapter 8:

Punishments

There is one aspect of parenthood, and child-rearing, that adds to the difficulty of the task due to the ever-changing social expectations and expert opinions. As children ourselves, we most likely heard the warnings of what we would consider now to be extreme punishment. One of these may include being spanked with a parent's hand or with a spoon. The punishments may also include physically washing a child's mouth out with soap, in addition to physical labor and denying the child dinner until their behavior improves.

Although some parents have been retroactively reprimanded for their punishment methods in the past, it is difficult to in fact blame them for their faulty methods. During the mid-1980s, there was not as much research into how the punishment methods of parents affect the psychological and emotional development of the child.

Thankfully, since the 1990s but especially since the turn of the millennium, child psychologists, social workers, and other medical professionals have spent many resources in trying to develop a philosophy of punishment and discipline for children that does not stunt or negatively affect their emotional or psychological development (Healthy Children, n.d.).

In recent years, many parents shy away from using the term punishment and discipline, as they believe that it is necessarily linked to the more extreme and damaging forms of punishment that have been seen in the past. However, what punishment and discipline truly entails is how the parents are to correct a child's behavior, and educate the child's correct expectations of how their behavior should be. Therefore, just as the methods of punishment and discipline have developed over the years, the definition of the terms have also developed. This distinction is to be made because throughout the rest of the chapter, it should be clear that when we refer to punishment and discipline, we are meaning this latter and more contemporary definition of the terms; that is a more gentle and educational approach to correcting bad or incorrect behavior.

So, how are parents today supposed to punish and show their child that their behavior is unacceptable without having the damaging effects that the previous generations punishment style has had?

The past 30 years of research into punishment methods have yielded 10 ways or steps through which parents can educate and discipline their children in a productive and gentle way.

Show and Tell

Perhaps the first way to gear poor behavior into more acceptable behavior is to model the desired behavior yourself. Many times children will feel left out or isolated in their own homes, as they know that they do not understand or know as much as their siblings or their parents do. For this reason, they may feel as though they are getting picked on or singled out when it is time for their behavior to be rectified.

For this reason, if they see and recognize their parents and siblings to follow the same sort of regulation in their behavior, while upholding the same sort of expectations, the child will most likely understand why their behavior is not acceptable and will therefore be less likely to exhibit that behavior.

For example, if one of your house rules is that before your child gets to play on the weekend, they must make their bed, it would be best for them to see that you ask their siblings that they must also make their bed before moving on with the day.

Set Limits and Give Consequences

Another way to help ensure acceptable behavior from your children is to set limits ahead of time. I am quite sure you give consequences if these limits are broken or passed. For example, if the child is coloring, some of the limits you can give is that they are only to be coloring for a specific time or only coloring on the page given.

Then, once the limits are set, you can then give consequences ahead of time so the child knows what to expect if their behavior does not match the limits. For example, if the child throws a tantrum after your set time of coloring is over, a possible consequence could be that they do not get to color the next day. Whereas, if the limit was that they must only color on the page given, yet they colored on the floor or the table, then a possible consequence could be that they get their crayons taken away.

An important thing to remember when setting limits and giving consequences to certain tasks is that the limit and the consequences need to be realistic and match with the activity. For example, if you set the limit that they can only color with the red crayon, that limit may hinder your child's enjoyment of the task, therefore encouraging poor behavior. Alternatively, if you give the consequence that your child does not get a treat later on in the day if they color on the table, you are not allowing the consequence to be immediate, therefore hindering their understanding of cause and effect.

Another important thing to remember is to ensure that you follow through with the consequences. If your adherence to the consequences is not consistent, then your child's behavior will not be consistent, and their knowledge as to why their behavior is incorrect in the first place will not be developed. Therefore, make sure that the consequences and the limits that you said are ones that you are comfortable sticking to.

Listen

One way to help you become more comfortable in setting limits, giving consequences, and overall learning how to discipline your child in a way that encourages understanding is to listen to your child.

There will undoubtedly be times through your journey of parenthood where you will ask your child to do something, and they will disagree or simply not do the task. In addition, this refusal to act will rarely be silent. One benefit of children is that they are incredibly honest and vocal about their discontent.

While some parents ignore when their child vocalizes their discontents, it is important to actually listen and pay attention to what your child is saying, or what they are trying to say. If you listen closely to what your child is saying and try to communicate with you during these instances of refusing to act, you will learn where their knowledge and understanding is lacking in listening to you. Through this discovery, you will be able to focus on those areas or gaps in their knowledge and therefore will be able to better educate your child as to why their actions were unacceptable.

Give Your Child Attention

One of the most common explanations as to why children act out is because they are trying to get the attention of their parents or the attention of someone else in the room. Additionally, similar to ensuring you are listening to what your child is saying during their refusal to listen, it is important that you give attention to them.

Generally, there are two ways that giving your child attention can help to avoid unacceptable behavior. First, you can ensure that your child knows that no matter what you are doing, your attention will always go to them when they ask for it. By doing so, you are letting your child know that there is no reason to act out in order to get your attention. The second way that giving attention can help to curb bad behavior is to pay attention and watch your child after you ask them to do something. If you ask them to do something, then walking away from the fact that they are not being supervised may encourage them to act inappropriately or to simply not do what they were asked.

Therefore, by asking them to do something, then ensuring that they know that you are there to supervise them, they are more likely to follow through with the request. One reason that it will encourage them to follow through is that they will want to impress you with how well they listened and how well the task was completed.

It may be difficult to remember, but it is important to know that your child does not want to be noticed for the state of being bad. They want you to notice them be good, and one way of getting bad attention is to behave acceptably.

Catch Them Being Good

Stemming from this previous step, an important way to curb and prevent poor behavior from your children is to catch them being good. Children who are only given attention when they are doing something bad are more likely to do bad things in order for them to get the attention they want. Children do not understand the difference between positive or negative attention, therefore if they are only given attention when they behave poorly, then they are more likely to behave poorly, as they believe that is the only way for them to get attention.

However, if you give your child attention when they are being good and not when they are behaving poorly, you are allowing your child to develop the skill of being able to discern and differentiate between positive attention and negative attention. By giving your child attention when they are being good, it also teaches your child that they do not have to behave poorly in order to get your attention. It also shows that if you reward them for behaving well, especially when they believe that you are not watching, it will encourage them to behave properly even without your supervision.

Know When to Say Nothing

As a parent, it may seem as though you are constantly warning your children of possible consequences, stopping them from doing something bad, or consistently explaining to them the cause-and-effect relationship between their actions and the results of their actions.

If you consistently warn your child of the consequences to their actions, or if you constantly repeat yourself as to how you expect them, you are not allowing your child to develop their own understanding and knowledge of what proper and improper behavior is. It is important that you give your child the opportunity to show you that they are able to recall the warned consequences of their actions. For this reason, it can be beneficial for you to not always repeat the possible punishment of your child's actions. Rather, give your child the chance to show you whether or not they understand what the expected behavior is in a certain situation; in turn, this shows you that they are improving their cognitive development.

Let Things Unfold on Their Own

Along the same lines of knowing when not to speak up, it is important to know when to allow negative consequences to unfold naturally. The exception to this of course is if the consequence of their poor behavior is something that can seriously harm your child. However, if the consequence of their action is one that you have told them repeatedly, or is one that will not result in a severe physical or emotional injury, like a broken bone, you should try to allow things to unfold as they would naturally.

In doing so, you are helping to show your child to important truths. The first is that you are a voice of authority and experience, and that you are not simply warning them because you do not want them to do an action—you are warning them for their own safety. The second is that consequences are a natural part and result of their actions. One important aspect of child-rearing is to help them understand that their actions have consequences, whether the consequences be positive or negative in the end. This knowledge is one that is developed through their own experiences.

Additionally, allowing consequences to happen naturally is also a way of disciplining your child without being the dreaded bad guy. If you consistently step in before a negative consequence happens naturally, then you may be seen as the negative consequence in your child's eyes. However, if you warn your child of the consequences then allow them to happen naturally, you are then seen as a hero, as you can come in and help your child feel better after the negative consequence happens.

This method of discipline, in addition to the one above of knowing when to stay quiet, is meant to be used in conjunction with others and not solely on their own. In the end, children need to learn from their own experiences in addition to understanding that you are an individual that should be listened to.

Prepare for Pushback

No matter how you choose to punish or discipline your children, you must remember that there will be pushback and resistance. No matter how understanding and empathetic you are to your child, or no matter how reasonable your requests or expectations of their behavior are, your child will try to test the limits of their own autonomy and pushback against either your request or your punishment.

Do not forget that most instances of poor or unacceptable behavior are not exhibited on purpose. Rather, they are usually done because your child does not understand what is expected of them, even if you've told them before. For this reason, you must try to remember to not take it personally when your child disobeys, does not listen, or behaves poorly. In fact, if you explode in your reaction, your child is more likely to not listen to the words you say to them, as was discussed in the previous chapters on listening and communication.

As hard as it may be, it is important to keep a level head, and I am sure you talk to your child on their level and in a way that they will understand, not in a way that intimidates them or scares them. These latter forms of communication are less likely to yield desired results.

Keep Unacceptable Behavior Within Its Own Limits

Another important aspect that you must remember when it comes to your children behaving badly, and assigning a proper and realistic consequence to the unacceptable behavior, is to keep bad behavior within its own limits.

As alluded to in the above disciplinary suggestions, when your child exhibits bad behavior, it does not necessarily mean that they are a bad child. For this reason, it is important to keep the consequences of the bad behavior within the limits and scope of the bad behavior itself. If the consequences and warnings that you give in an attempt to curb unacceptable behavior go beyond the scope of what makes sense, you may encourage the misconception that your child is a bad child.

It is perhaps best to explain that suggestion through examples. Let us say for example that your child colors on the wall after you specifically told them to only color on the designated piece of paper or area. If the consequences and punishment for this inappropriate behavior is that your child gets yelled at, does not get any treats that day, and does not get to watch any television that day, your child may develop a sense that they are not a good person, as the punishment for their inappropriate behavior is so much larger then behavior itself. Therefore, to keep the unacceptable behavior within its own limit, a possible consequence would be to have your child, with your help of course, wash the wall or the floor on which they colored. In this way, you are teaching your child that there are negative consequences and expectations to their inappropriate behavior. You should also show them that their one and singular instance of inappropriate behavior does not negatively affect their general daily routine.

Redirect Poor Behavior and Encourage Time-Outs

One more suggestion that medical professionals suggest when it comes to disciplining your children is that you try to redirect the poor behavior and encourage time-outs or periods of calm. Again, in keeping with the theme of only punishing the inappropriate and unacceptable behavior itself, you may find it beneficial and helpful to try and redirect inappropriate behavior toward acceptable behavior.

One way of doing so would be to frame your punishment or consequences as productive activities. For instance, teaching your child to clean after they have made a mess is one way of creating a consequence that is productive.

Another way of helping to curb inappropriate behavior, without necessarily over exaggerating the consequence, is to encourage periods of calm. Unacceptable behavior usually rears its head when the child is already tired or frustrated. Therefore, by looking out for the signs of your child being tired and frustrated, and redirecting these negative emotions to participating and calming activities, you can preemptively and proactively avoid negative and unacceptable behavior.

* * *

As you can see through these 10 previous examples, the philosophy behind disciplining and punishing children is to ensure their understanding of what makes acceptable and unacceptable behavior. It also shows that the methods focus on creatively or proactively setting up the child to behave properly so as to avoid poor behavior later on. However, it is inevitable that children will misbehave. For this reason, the new philosophy of disciplining and punishing your children is not aimed at reprimanding them for the behavior but more to educate them as to why their behavior was wrong and giving realistic consequences.

One of the issues to the "old way" of punishing children was that the punishment and consequences were unrealistic. For example, if you are to lie as an adult there is a large chance that you will not be spanked with a belt; along the same lines if you swear as an adult, your mouth will not be washed out with soap.

If we take into consideration the above steps and methods, you can see that the consequences and punishments that are given for child poor behavior logically follow from the poor behavior itself. For example, if you warn your child beforehand to not jump on the couch as they will fall off and hurt themselves, the consequence that follows if they were to jump on the couch is that they will most likely fall off and hurt themselves. In allowing for the consequence to happen, your child will recognize that the consequence you warned them of came true and therefore teach them in the process why their action was incorrect in the first place. Allow us to use one more example to really clarify the picture. Let us say, for example, that you are trying to teach your child to not lie, as lying will lead to others not trusting them or not believing them. These are two consequences of lying that will generally come true whether the individual is a child or if they are an adult. If your child continues to not tell the truth, and as a consequence your actions show that you do not trust them, they will recognize that the lying was incorrect.

The important takeaway from this chapter is that disciplining and punishing your children is not to be a fear. Disciplining and punishing your children does not necessarily include those extreme forms that were practiced over 50 years ago. Consider disciplining and punishing your children as a way of educating them into the different expectations of their behavior and helping them to understand the natural consequences of their behavior. In that regard, you are teaching them discipline, cause and effect, and allowing them to develop a healthy emotional response to negative consequences, as they understand that just because they did something wrong does not mean that they are a bad person (Healthy Children, n.d.).

Of course, disciplining children differs as the child grows, develops, and learns new ways of disobeying you and testing their limits. Help Guide#1 goes through some tips for disciplining children of different ages and what kind of limits testing you will most likely find.

Chapter 9:

Dealing With External Factors

Throughout the book, there has been allusions to how the state of and situations in the world can affect the communication and relationship between you and your children; however, this chapter deals with it directly as it brings all of the information within the book to a climax.

It is not necessarily true that all conflicts within the parent-child relationship stem from internal conflict. Instead, external factors to the relationship, such as the different stresses from the world placed on each individual person, can breed and encourage a poor relationship. For example, how often do you find that when you are stressed, frustrated, or flustered, your willingness to listen to others decreases? Furthermore, how often do you find that when you are not feeling your best, your communication skills hinder?

Within the past one to two years, the largest and most influential external stressor that is common to all parents in the world is the current pandemic and the associated regulations (Brunelli, 2020). This pandemic has forced schools to close and companies to distribute their employees back to their homes to work. As a result the home that was usually full of people only in the mornings and evenings is now at all times of the day.

Also, this pandemic, in disallowing people from gathering, closing food establishments, and shutting down social events has taken away many stress-relieving techniques for people. Both adults and children find themselves at a loss for how they can cope with the stress of changing the world.

As a result, the stress level of the individual has risen. Unfortunately, when individuals feel more stressed, they tend to disregard the feelings and emotions of others.

Consequently, many families are now finding themselves in a tension-filled household, where the parents find their children are acting out, and where children feel that their parents simply don't understand what they are going through.

To add to the stress of being individually overwhelmed, many parents are finding it more difficult to balance their work, home, and personal lives. This is because in the past there were designated times and areas for each part of your life. For example, you would leave the house to go to work, you would come home to be with your family, and you would leave the house again to indulge in your personal life with your friends. For your children, their stressors are the same. They would go to school to identify their school life, they would come home to spend time with you, and they would leave the house again to go play with their friends. However, now in both cases, the home is the center of all three aspects of life. This concentration and amalgamation of every aspect of everyone's life, has led to an increase in tension and stress between family members and overall within the household (Brunelli, 2020).

How to Get Through Rough Times

Fortunately, although many feel as though you are alone in the chaos, you are not. Most every family around the world has felt the effects of the recent pandemic and economic issues that have resulted from it.

Also, never think that you are not even alone within your own household. Your entire household has most likely been affected in the same ways as you have. Therefore, rather than seeing working at home and studying at home as an obstacle or a struggle to get through, view it as an opportunity to come closer and create a stronger bond between you and your child or children.

Of course, in order to do this, there are some suggestions that experts have put forth to help ease the transition and to smooth over any conflicts or frustration that may arise (Leonhardt, 2020).

Keep Open Lines of Honest Communication With Everyone

The first and perhaps most important step or suggestion to ensuring that your house is a formidable environment for you to work, for your children to study, and for you to take advantage of the situation to become closer to your children, is that you should keep open lines of honest communication between everyone in the household.

That is to say that when anyone in your house is feeling stressed, overwhelmed, happy, nervous, worried, or whatever other emotion, that they feel safe and never judged when they speak about it. Many reasons why individuals do not speak out about their anxieties or worries is because they do not want to feel judged or made to feel stupid for feeling in such a way. However, it has been proven time and time again that by letting these feelings of anxiety linger and grow within yourself that the individual can develop anxiety or other mental disorders.

For that reason, it is important that your children know that they can come to you when they do not like what is going on, and that you equally are allowed to go to them when you do not like what they are doing.

However, it is also important that you keep an honest line of communication open with yourself. As a parent, many of us tend to hide our emotions so as to not burden our children with them or have our children see us as someone who is imperfect. However, in times like these, it is important for your children to witness you stealing the same negative emotions as they are feeling. This is because it will allow them to recognize that they are not alone in their own feelings of anxiety and frustration, and that you are someone who they can go to when they need to vent their anxieties to.

Set Limits and Create Rules Together

Another suggestion that can help ease the tension throughout these days of chaos and confusion is to use the open line of communication to set limits and create rules. Perhaps once a week or once a month—depending on how long it takes for there to be some feelings of normalcy—come together as a family and dictate the expectations that each of you have for each other throughout the day, designate times of play and activity, and generally come up with rules to help structure the day.

For example, one of your rules could be that when you are working, the children can only come to you if they need to. Alternatively, a rule set forth by your child could be that they do not want to be focused on schoolwork all day.

By sitting out limits, rules, and expectations—and consistently going back and evaluating these expectations—you can help to create an environment that everyone is comfortable with and where everyone's needs are met.

Focus on Quality Over Quantity

Another way to help redirect the stress and pressures that come along with everyone in your household working at home is to focus on quality over quantity. That is to say, try to focus on the quality of work and time that you spend with your family over the quantity of time that you spend on your work or your family.

To break this down, let us look at each half individually. You may find it more useful to designate a certain time of day where you are working, and that your child is not to bother you, rather than puttering around all day doing work here and there. For example, you may want to designate the first half of the day on work, and designate the second half of the day for errands or fun activities. The same philosophy can be applied, generally speaking, to your children's online schooling. Speak with your child's teacher to see if your child is able to only be online for the first half of the day, and make sure that your child is doing their work within this first half of the day.

By designating your day into times of work and play, you are helping your child, and yourself, to have a structured routine. This will, in turn, help you cope with the day ahead.

On the other hand, you can apply the same philosophy to spending time with your family. Be sure that when you are spending time with your children, whether it be educational learning, simply hanging out, or playing, that your child knows they are the main priority. It will confuse your child even more if they see you home all day with them but not have any sort of closer connection to you. Therefore, be sure that when you are spending time with your family, that is all that you are doing. By doing so, you will get more feelings of fulfillment and satisfaction than you would if you tried to multitask between your work and your children sporadically throughout the day.

Create a Positive Routine and Environment

An imperative step in making sure that the stress of staying home does not interfere with your everyday routine and how you treat one another is to create a positive environment. There are a few different ways you can create and maintain a positive environment while being overwhelmed and stressed. The two most beneficial and effective ways that parents have recently found to maintain their household as a peaceful and positive environment, among the craziness and hectic changes in their life, is to designate one area of the house as the negative zone and to adopt a daily routine of positive affirmations. Let us talk about the former first.

A negative zone is an area of the house where individuals can go when they are feeling stressed, overwhelmed, or frustrated. By designating a zone, you are acknowledging that feelings of frustration and anger are natural emotions to have, especially considering the circumstances. However, there is a time and place to deal with these negative emotions safely and constructively. The negativity zone in your house can be a room or another floor of your house where you have some designated activities that can help calm your family members, or yourself, when these feelings of frustration arise. For example, there could be a television within the room with some humorous movies so you are able to unwind and detach yourself from your work or your child from their schoolwork. This room can also contain coloring supplies, a yoga mat, something to play music on, or generally anything that can help to take your frustration away and allow you to reenter the family home in a more positive mood.

The second way to create a positive environment throughout the home is to adopt a practice and routine of positive affirmations. Positive affirmations are short phrases or sentences that have a positive tone to them and that have the power to inspire and motivate you to do a certain task.

Positive affirmations have been proven to help keep individuals motivated and happy in a variety of stressful situations. For example, individuals who have been traumatized or who are trying to heal are known to use positive affirmations to help keep them on track to their goal. On the other hand, positive affirmations have already been proven effective in the household, as they can help keep the individuals in the house motivated and happy. Therefore, it would make sense that positive affirmations can help keep the household motivated in stressful and chaotic times such as these.

To adopt such a routine is not difficult. All it requires is for you and your family to come together in the morning, and choose one or more positive affirmation for the day to be based on. Then, once the affirmations have been chosen, have each member of your family write it out on a piece of paper a few times over. Then, post the individual pieces of paper all over the house in places where they will be seen on a consistent basis. For example, on a doorway that is walked through often, the edge of a computer screen, a mirror, or even hidden in some of your children's toys. The repetitive reading and noticing of the positive affirmation will help to keep you and your family focused on the goal of the day and being motivated.

* * *

Ultimately, the key to insuring a calm environment throughout these crazy and tumultuous world events is to keep an open line of communication with your children, and to try and keep them as positive as possible.

Admittedly, the tasks are easier said than done. However, it is important to remember that these times are only temporary. However, the lessons you learn and the progress you make to bring you and your children closer will last forever. Additionally, they will give you the tool to better cope when similar stresses for world events happen again, although we hope these are tools that you never have to use again (Leonhardt, 2020).

Conclusion

To bring this book to a close, there are three major aspects that can be improved on to bring about an overall improvement in your relationship between your child or children and yourself as a parent. Namely, these areas are listening, communication, and understanding.

Although there are two sides of communication, two sides of listening, and two sides of understanding, as a parent, it is your responsibility to embody the behavior you want to see in your child. When it comes to mending the relationship, increasing more effective communication, and all around bringing about a greater sense of understanding between you and your child—especially when it comes to younger children who are learning and developing their listening and communication skills—verbally telling them what to do is not enough. You must show them with your own actions.

By embodying the behavior you want to see, you are showing your child that the behavior is expected by all individuals and persons in the relationship and family. Therefore, although the list of exercises and activities is to encourage better listening and better communication from your child, the most important takeaway from this book is that communication, listening, and understanding is a bilateral relationship. The responsibility is not simply on your child but also on how you approach the situation.

Although the current and new state of society has brought on new levels and types of stress and conflict between parent and child, it can also be used and seen as an opportunity to improve the relationship between parent and child. The more time that is being spent with your children is not necessarily bringing up new conflicts; rather, it is highlighting and exasperating already present issues. Therefore, rather than blaming the current state of the world for the increased stress, try to consider the current situation as an opportunity to better and mend your relationship with your child.

By putting the effort in now to help your child communicate and listen better to you, you are not only improving your own relationship with them, but you are also helping them to develop proper and well-established skills in the areas of communication, listening, and understanding. Skills that will help them be a more successful person in society later on in life.

Help Guide #1:

Potential Challenges by Age

Infants

Children in the infant stage are learning by watching you. They are constantly absorbing everything you are doing and are learning how to act from how you interact with them and others.

For this reason, it is important that you make sure you act appropriately in front of them. This means that you should try your best to not lose your temper with them or others while in their presence. Furthermore, you should try to keep a level head when someone in front of you is losing control of their own temper. By doing so, you can preemptively teach them more constructive ways of dealing with changes in mood other than having a tantrum.

At this age, your child will want to explore and touch everything—even things they are not supposed to. Therefore, it is imperative that you remove those items that you do not want them to touch right away, so they do not think that it is okay for them to be touched.

This time in your child's development is when they are beginning to form words and understand short and simple instructions. So, keep your instructions to them simple to understand and direct to the point. Furthermore, you should always be talking to your child in a positive way. When you use phrases like "Mommy/Daddy is always here," "Use your words," and letting them make their own noises back to you, whatever they are, you are getting a step ahead of any communication issues as you are encouraging them to speak and praising them for communicating with you.

There are no conventional poor behaviors to expect from your child, nor are there any tips for punishment, as your child is still very young. However, at this point in your child's development, it is important to stay as positive as you can, and try to avoid using negative language altogether unless absolutely needed. When negative language or "punishment" is needed, try to use it in a productive way so as to simply redirect their attention and distract them from the situation, rather than actually punishing them. This will help you stay away from any unnecessary tantrums and feelings of anxiety within your child at this age (Healthy Children, n.d.).

Toddlers

At this age, your child is beginning to understand what behaviors are unallowed and unacceptable and which are allowed and acceptable. However, they may still be learning why such behaviors have different allowances.

For this reason, it is important that you praise and make sure that your child is aware of when they are doing a good job or behaving properly. Alternatively, it is equally important for you to let them know when their behavior is poor. To be clear, letting them know and understanding which behavior is good and which is bad is not a form of oppressive discipline that many parents are afraid of falling into. As your toddler is still learning, they must be told when they are not behaving properly, as they may know they are.

By this time, your child will have developed a pattern for their personality and behavior, meaning that there are likely to be known triggers for their poor behavior. For this reason, try to avoid those triggers, or prepare yourself to experience them or relieve a tantrum early. For example, be sure to have snacks with you if you are expecting to leave the house for a long time, do not get rid of daily naps too soon, try not to push them by too long, and be sure to have any comforting items for your child close by if needed.

Perhaps the most common poor behavior that is exhibited by a child in the toddler age range is what is known as a temper tantrum. These are times when your child is overflowing with feelings and emotions that they are not able to name or communicate with you, resulting in an outburst of tears, throwing toys, or other exaggerated and dramatic behavior.

Do not be afraid or ashamed if your toddler experiences a tantrum. It is a natural part of growing up and it is how you treat a tantrum that will set the tone for the future ones.

Tips for Tantrums

- Do Not Ignore Your Child

Many old stories say that if you ignore your child when they are acting out, like in a temper tantrum, the belief is that your child will realize that they are not getting your attention and will stop. However, this belief misses the whole point of why toddlers have tantrums; it is to get your attention. Tantrums are rarely thrown just for fun; there is usually a reason. Most often, it is because your child is feeling something that they cannot put into words, thereby looking for your attention and guidance to help them feel better. Therefore, the first step in properly dealing with a tantrum is to give your child attention.

- Do Not Give in to the Demands

While it is important that you give your child attention, it is equally important that you do not give in to the demand that your toddler is asking for. For example, if they are asking for a toy or a treat that you said no to.

This is an important step to relieving tantrums, and a step that must be done consistently, as you do not want your child to use tantrums as a way of getting their way.

- Find the Root of the Problem

Next, try to find the root of the problem, tantrum, or generally bad behavior. Are they hungry and that is why they are so insistent on the treat? Are they bored shopping and that is why they want the toy to play with?

By finding the root of the problem, you can identify the feeling that they may be feeling but are unable to communicate.

- Try to Help Them to Calmly Communicate

Once you find the root of the problem, you can help to guide your toddler toward being able to communicate their feelings in a calm way.

Talk to your child in a calm voice, and ask them questions that help them get to the right words. There is a good chance that your toddler understands the words hungry, thirsty, etc., however, they may be having trouble realizing that those are the feelings they are experiencing.

Once they are calm and are able to communicate how they feel, they are more likely to be receptive to a way of soothing their feelings without the thing they wanted. You can give them a healthy snack that you brought with you or at the very least distract them with some sort of toy.

- Physically Soothe Them

One very important part of dealing with a tantrum is that you must physically and emotionally calm your child down. They are likely feeling warm, are shaking, perhaps their stomach hurts, or they may even have a headache from screaming and crying.

For this reason, take hold of your child firmly but gently, pick them up, and give them a hug. The pressure of the hug or the warmth of your touch will help them to redirect their attention from what is making them upset and to something calm and safe.

Furthermore, sometimes a tantrum is thrown simply because they want to be held, therefore picking them up, rubbing their back, and holding them tight will be sufficient in making them feel calm.

Keep in mind that no matter the age, your child is a small human; therefore, the same calming techniques used for adults to make them feel better when they are sad can be used for your child.

* * *

The key to handling toddlers is to help them understand that there is always a way to calmly communicate what they feel and what they do not understand. It is your role to help them develop these communication skills, so as to avoid acting out in a desperate attempt to relieve their stress.

Preschool-Aged Children

At this age, your child is beginning to understand why certain behaviors are wrong and why certain behaviors are acceptable. However, they may still try to test the limits of their bad behavior, in addition to a time still not understanding why certain behaviors are wrong.

Therefore, for preschool-aged children, it is important to remember that they are still in the learning process. Try not to take it personally if you find that your child is behaving badly on a consistent basis or in a similar way. Perhaps tackle that behavior itself rather than drawing it out and making it a generalized problem. Maybe it is something about the situation that consistently makes your child feel uncomfortable in a way that they have yet to be soothed and relieved from.

Unfortunately, it is this age where your child will interact with other children on a regular basis. Therefore, the behavior and actions of other children will likely influence the actions of your own child. Make sure that you are explaining and reiterating what proper behavior is and explaining to them that other children may not have the same rules as they do, but they are still to follow your rules.

Furthermore, this is also the age where children tend to purposely misbehave as a way of challenging their parents. In these cases some parents will have no choice but to discipline their children. For those parents, it is important to remember to punish the behavior itself, not the child in general. This means that the punishment should fit the poor behavior and should not make your child feel as though they are a bad person for doing the bad behavior.

One way that child experts have suggested to further solidify responsibility, communication, and overall good behavior is to invite your chat to take part in some age-appropriate chores. When children have responsibilities, they feel as though they are being trusted and are proud in the work they have done. Therefore, children who have small responsibilities that they enjoy doing are more likely to not be affected by the poor behavior of other children and are more likely to not need to be punished for poor behavior.

Older Children

However, as your child develops out of preschool and into older childhood, it becomes harder to explain the way and justify poor behavior by saying that they are still learning.

For this reason, it is during these older years of childhood where you may need to make your punishments slightly more severe in order to drive home the message that the behavior is bad.

It is still important to make the punishments fit the poor behavior and not an overarching generalized punishment. Moreover, make sure you are focusing on your child and understanding why their behavior is wrong, rather than simply making them feel bad for the behavior (Healthy Children, n.d.).

Games to Help With Listening and

Communication

Harkening back specifically to "Chapter 2: How to Get Your Kids to Listen to You," one way to help improve your child's listening skills is to turn listening into a game. Depending on what the issue is concerning why you believe your child does not listen to you, turning listening into a game can have different benefits.

First, if you think that your child has to develop better listening skills, the games can help you focus your child's attention and develop the mental skills required to listen properly in a fun and entertaining way, one that makes them feel as though they are simply having fun and not learning.

Secondly, if you believe the reason that your child does not listen to you is because they feel as though listening is simply not a fun thing to do, these games can help them feel closer to you and show them that listening can be used in ways others than just listening to what you ask them to in everyday situations.

Third, not only do these listening games help to develop the listening faculties and skills, but many of these games involve an aspect of reciprocal communication, therein allowing them to develop and improve upon their communication skills as well.

Lastly, keep in mind that these games, at their most basic and simplest levels, are just that: games. They are meant to be fun. Try not to focus too much on the development part of these activities, if you do, you may be putting more pressure on your child which will push them backward in their development. Rather, it is important to keep the mood light and really highlight the bonding and fun that the two, or more, of you are having (Miller, 2021).

Listening and Communication Games

What Time Is it, Mr. Wolf?

What time is it, Mr. Wolf? allows your child to develop listening skills as they have to hear what others are saying from a distance, in addition to following the instructions provided.

To play, you first have to have at least three people, but for this one, the more the better. Therefore, this game is best to be played if you have multiple children or a group of children.

The game starts by designating one person as Mr. Wolf; this person then goes a little ways away, but still in earshot of the others, and turns their back to the rest of the group. The other children shout the question "What time is it, Mr. Wolf?" The wolf then replies with a number from 1-12 signifying a time of day. The other players then take that many steps toward the wolf. After a few rounds of this, the children move closer and closer to the wolf. Eventually, when the wolf feels and hears that the others are close enough, the next time they ask their question, the wolf is to shout, "lunch time!" and turn to chase after the other children. Whoever the wolf tags first is then the wolf, and the game begins again.

This game helps both the wolf and the other children, as both roles and players in the game must use their ears to either hear the number of steps to take or how close the other players are. To make the game more challenging and fun, play the game outside so the children must actively block out other outside noises; or allow the wolf to whisper, "lunch time," requiring the other children to listen more attentively.

Finish the Story

This game is one that is quite simple and does not require any body movements or physical activity. This makes the game one that can be used to calm the child before their bedtime or in other situations.

Generally, this game involves you telling a story while taking turns telling what happens. Specifically, how you play is you first choose whether the designated words to be said will be one, two, or three words; for the sake of this example, we will use one word. Then after choosing who goes first, that person begins the story with one word: "once." The next player in the game then says one word that relates to the first in an attempt to tell a story. The third player then says another word, and so on and so forth, until sentences, ideas, and a story are formed. Although this game is more fun when there are more players, this game can be played with as little as two people.

This game requires the players to pay attention to the words that came before them and answer with a related word. In this way, the game helps your child to develop their listening skills and their communication skills as they must answer and reply appropriately.

A variation of the game allows each player to say one sentence rather than one word. However, this is a version for older children or those who have more advanced communication skills, as it requires them to develop an entire thought rather than one word.

Emotional Charades

Emotional charades is a version of charades that is focused on helping your child communicate important developmental concepts without words. The basic game of charades happens where one person chooses a phrase or word then acts the word out, without using vocal cues or communication, for the others to guess. Following this, whoever guesses the acted-out phrase correctly is the next person to choose a phrase.

Where the original game allows individuals to choose words from categories like films, books, TV shows, or people, emotional charades is based on different emotions or emotional concepts.

To play, first write down, on different pieces of paper, a collection of emotions, emotional concepts, or emotionally related words, and put them in a small bowl for the players to pick from. After designating one person to go first, have them choose a piece of paper out of the bowl. The player then has to act out the word or phrase using their body and props but no words or sounds.

This game, whether played with two people or more, helps your child to communicate as they must try to share a message without using words. This will not only show them the importance and convenience of using words while communicating, but it will also help them to hone their nonverbal communication skills. This game also helps to develop listening skills as the sitting players must "listen" to the nonverbal cues given by the other player (Helleran, 2020).

Pictionary

Similar to emotional charades, Pictionary allows your child practice and hone their nonverbal communication skills, as they must draw what their word or phrase is for the other players to guess.

The basis for this game is similar to above as well. Before the game begins, you must first write down or choose a selection of different words into a bowl; for this, as there is no theme, you can also use clues for the actual game of Pictionary, or you can create your own. You then have one person drawing the word, while the others guess what they are trying to draw. The individual who guesses correctly draws next.

While this game is largely focused on developing the communication skills of your child, this game can also be used to improve their listening skills as well; especially if you have multiple people guessing what the image is—or is trying to be—then the person drawing must listen attentively to hear the answer through a field of noise and wrong answers. They must also be able to discern between which voice belongs to which person, so as to accurately assign a winner.

Telephone

Telephone, the classic game from childhood, was the epitome of hilarity and frustration for many children. This game involves the first player to whisper a sentence or phrase into the ear of the next player. That person then repeats exactly what they hear to the next player by whispering in their ear. The games move forward in the same way until that original person receives the message, who then repeats exactly what they heard out loud. Their sentence is then compared to how closely it resembles this original message, which is almost never the same as the original. It makes it an easy and fun game for multiple ages.

Although this game is better to be played with at least three people, in fact the more the better, it can be played with just two. Rather than have the second person say the phrase out loud, have them repeat it to the first person, and make the first person say the new message out loud.

This game helps to develop the listening and communication skills of your child because it brings to light how easily communication can fail or be manipulated from one person to another. It can also show your child how listening is an important part of the message/sender process, as what you hear dictates what you think the message is.

To make this game easier for the first person, and to take the pressure off of your child to come up with sentences and phrases, you can preemptively write a collection of well-known phrases and short simple sentences that can be used as the message. This preparation can also help you ensure that the original message is one that makes sense and is not distorted from the beginning, as that would be ineffective toward the goal of the game (Miller, 2021)

Reverse Marco Polo

Marco Polo is a game that nearly everyone is familiar with. It usually involves one person, who has their eyes closed or is blindfolded, shouting out the word "Marco!" The other players then respond with "Polo!" The blindfolded person then tries to find and tag one of the other players based on where they hear the voice coming from. The tagged player then becomes the blindfolded player.

Although this game is usually played with a large group of people, and outdoors, there is a "reverse" version that can be played indoors and with only two players. For this version, the blindfolded player stands in the middle of the room, while the other player walks around the room making noises either with objects or their own voice. The blindfolded player must then turn to face where they believe the noises to be coming from and name the object they think is being used.

As such, your child will consequently learn to understand how different noises work in their specific direction, in addition to heightening their listening skills without being able to see where the noise was coming from.

Silent Communication

The silent communication game is one that not only allows your child to develop their communication and listening skills but also gives you some quiet time within the house throughout the day.

To play this game, designate a specific amount of time during the day where there is to be no talking of any kind. This does not mean that it has to be completely silent, nor does this mean that you have to ignore or not communicate with your child. Rather, go on with your regular activities throughout the day but remove the verbal communication. Try to go as long as you can by communicating through body language and natural sounds rather than words and phrases.

This "game" helps your child to develop their communication skills in a similar way that emotional charades and Pictionary does. However, it also highlights, for the child, the importance of natural noises and forces them to pay attention to communication that is audible but not verbal. For example, snapping fingers, hearing footsteps, or hearing different sounds from another room.

One Step, Two Steps, Three Steps

This game is not a version of another childhood game but rather a more entertaining version of asking your child to do things. For this game, you generally take turns asking each other to do a series of small actions or tasks. The first task will be a simple one that can be done in "one step." The second task will have two steps, while the third will have three.

The goal of this activity is to have your child remember what you have said and complete the tasks in order and as you said them. Once they are done, it is their turn to do the same for you.

Be sure that the tasks you are saying are not complicated, nor are they like doing chores. This is meant to be a fun activity. This means that you can get your child to do anything as silly or ridiculous as you like, and they can do the same. For example, step one would be to hop on one leg five times, step two is to flap your arms and cluck like a chicken, and step three would be to turn your clothes around, do a dance, and sing a song.

Although this activity seems simple, it can help your child to develop their listening skills and cognitive skills to perform associated actions. By then asking you to do their own series of chosen activities, they are practicing their communication skills as they tell you what to do in different steps.

Listening Walk

This activity is one that helps your child to practice and develop their listening skills in addition to the skills needed to discern between different noises and increase their knowledge of noise direction and noise source.

For this activity, all that is needed is for you to simply go for a walk or play outside with your child. Then, as different sounds and noises are heard, take turns naming the noises that you hear.

If you want to make the game into a scavenger hunt, you can always make a list of predicted sounds that you have heard in the past and challenge your child to find those sounds on your walk.

Freeze Dance

This classic game is a way for your child to practice their listening skills while having fun and getting their heart rate up.

Generally, this game has you dancing with your child or children in different ways and however you like while music is playing. Then, at random times, pause the music, at which time you and your child are supposed to stop and freeze until the music starts to play again.

To make this a more difficult game, and one that challenges your child's hearing a little more, you can play and change the volume of the music from loud to soft and from soft to loud. This way, your child needs to listen closely to the music to know when to start or stop. Another version of this game is for you to not only stop and start the music but to change the music as well. Then, when the music begins again, they have to dance in a new way to the new music. In this way, you will help your child to develop cognitive skills associated with listening such as changing their behavior according to what they hear.

Instructive Drawing

Instructive drawing tests your child's memory and cognitive skills in addition to their listening skills. This is a rather simple game that does not require much if any physical exertion; therefore, it can be a game used to fill time during car rides, other instances of waiting, or when you want your child to stay calm.

To play, all your child needs is some crayons or markers, a piece of paper, and their listening skills. Ultimately, the goal of the game is to draw a story or pictures from what you are saying. You can either tell your child to draw something specific and in a certain color. Or you can be broader and tell them a general story, and have them draw pictures that tell the story how they understood it.

In the end, this game will not only help your child with their listening skills, but it will give you a glimpse into how your child is understanding what you say, and how they conceptualize the different objects in the story.

* * *

As you can see, these games are ones that can be used as tools to develop listening and communication skills, in addition to simply being a fun way to spend time with your kids.

However, take note that this list is far from being complete and exhaustive. There are quite literally hundreds of types, varieties, and versions of childhood games that can help your child to improve your communicative relationship. Many of them are ones that you are already familiar with or played as a child yourself, like, for example, "What time is it, Mr. Wolf?" However, the list above of games uses those that are the most popular and those that other parents and specialists have found most effective and fun for children to play, as they do not require much preparation or extra parts to use during play.

Help Guide #3:

Positive Affirmations for Parents

and Children

As mentioned in "Chapter 9: Dealing With External Factors," one way to maintain a positive, calm, and all-around better environment in the household is to adapt a positive affirmation daily routine. Especially with the chaos that is happening around the world, the structure of everyone's daily routines and the family unit itself has shifted. Now, everyone is being forced to work alongside each other in a confined space that you are not used to. Of course, being in such close quarters has led to some tensions being risen, tempers boiling over, and basic understanding and respect—on everyone's part—has been challenged. In the end, we lose sight of what is important: that is keeping each other strong and supported during times of stress. One way to do so is to adopt the positive affirmation routine.

Although described in previous chapters, it will be summarized here again. The point of a daily affirmation routine is to remind all people in the household what is truly important during these times, keep them motivated and positive, and encourage a healthy thriving environment. Every day, gather your family to choose one or two affirmations that stick out to them. You may even go as far as each person choosing their own each day. Then, write down each affirmation on a few different pieces of paper and post them throughout the house in places and on appliances where they will be seen. Throughout the day, when you find one, read it to yourself before leaving that area. Good places to hide the affirmations would be on the fridge, on the bathroom mirror, or on the computer screens where people are likely to get work done and potentially become frustrated.

Of course, making up your own affirmations can be a daunting task. For this reason, we have come up with a few here for you to choose from until your family is comfortable with finding or creating your own. These affirmations have been specifically developed to bring people together, reduce stress, bring smiles to your faces, and encourage closeness between family members.

- We are strong as a family.

- I am a great parent.

- I am a great child.

- I support my children to help them grow and develop.

- I support my mom and dad when they are stressed.

- I understand the stresses in my child's life and help them through it all.

- We learn and grow together as a family.

- We are always developing and becoming stronger as individuals and together.

- I am grateful for my family.

- I am willing to admit I am wrong.

- When something goes wrong, we seek to solve the problem together.

- I am confident in my role in the family.

- My role in the family is _____.

- I listen to my child when they speak.

- I respect and listen to what my mom and dad say.

- My child does not mean to challenge me.

- I do what is right for my family.

- We are a support system.

- We are there for each other.

- Keeping the family unit strong is key.

- I love my family.

- I am healthy and happy.

- I do not compare my family to others.

- I take the time I need to improve myself.

- Time-outs are helpful to gear negative emotions.

- I communicate with my family as much as possible.

- Sometimes, I cannot communicate my feelings, and that is okay.

- Make time to play.

- Life is more than working.

- We are successful as individuals and as a family.

- My family's health, including mine, is important.

- I do what it takes to keep my family safe and healthy.

- Everything we need, we can find in each other.

- Setbacks are learning experiences.

- I am constantly learning new things.

- Not all failures are negative experiences.

- Life is good for our family.

- Frustration is a productive emotion.

- Our home is a safe space.

- I am accepted and unjudged in my family.

- This too shall pass.

- Inconveniences are merely temporary.

- We will get through this.

- Struggles make us stronger.

- Stress will not break us.

- We enjoy spending time together.

- Alone time is okay.

- Discipline is productive not limiting.

- I am patient.

- I seek understanding if I do not understand.

- The past cannot be changed.

- We are ready for the future.

- Today will be a great day!

- I can do anything I set my mind to!

- I am in charge of my own behavior and attitude.

- I can go to my parents for help and guidance.

- I do not give up.

- My support system is strong.

- I am helping my children have bright futures.

- It is okay to be scared and worried in times like these.

- Our beliefs and faith give us power.

- We share our feelings openly with each other and without condescension or judgment.

- We are fair and equal people.

- Each person in our family has their own path.

- We work to reach and support each other's desires and goals.

- I mirror how I want to be treated to others.

- I give the love I want to receive.

- I am a positive person.

- I am raising strong children.

- I am comfortable with who I am.

- I am powerful in my mind and body.

- It is okay that I do not know.

References

Brunelli, L. (2020, October 30). The balancing Act: Working at home with kids. Retrieved February 2021, from https://www.verywellfamily.com/how-work-at-home-parents-can-achieve-balance-4126773

Bryant, A. (n.d.). How to be a better listener. Retrieved February 2021, from https://www.nytimes.com/guides/smarterliving/be-a-better-listener

CDC. (2019, November 05). Active listening. Retrieved February 2021, from https://www.cdc.gov/parents/essentials/communication/activelistening.html

Child Development. (2019, July 23). Feeling hopeless? Learn how to talk so your kids will listen. Retrieved February 2021, from https://childdevelopmentinfo.com/how-to-be-a-parent/communication/talk-to-kids-listen/#gs.wfychf

Communication Theory. (2014, July 07). Types of communication. Retrieved February 2021, from https://www.communicationtheory.org/types-of-communication/

EDUCBA. (2020, July 14). Types of Communication: 6 types of communication you must excel at. Retrieved February 2021, from https://www.educba.com/types-of-communication/

Halloran, J. (2020, July 22). Listening games for kids. Retrieved February 2021, from https://www.encourageplay.com/blog/listening-games-for-kids

Healthy Children. (n.d.). What's the best way to discipline my child? Retrieved February 2021, from https://www.healthychildren.org/English/family-life/family-dynamics/communication-discipline/Pages/Disciplining-Your-Child.aspx

Johansson, A. (2016, October 14). 5 reasons you're failing to communicate - and how to fix it. Retrieved February 2021, from https://www.businessinsider.com/5-reasons-youre-failing-to-communicate-and-how-to-fix-it-2016-10

John M. Grohol, P. (2016, May 17). 10 reasons you don't listen. Retrieved February 2021, from https://psychcentral.com/lib/10-reasons-you-dont-listen#2

Kline, J. (1996). *Listening Effectively* (pp. 29-44, Rep.). Air University Press. Retrieved February 28, 2021, from http://www.jstor.org/stable/resrep13885.11

Lee, K. (2020). Stressed kids: Signs and causes of childhood anxiety. Retrieved February 2021, from https://www.verywellfamily.com/how-to-spot-anxiety-and-stress-in-children-620518

Leonhardt, M. (2020, August 06). Lack of school and child care could mean losing 'a generation of working parents'. Retrieved February 2021, from https://www.cnbc.com/2020/08/06/lack-of-school-and-child-care-may-push-some-parents-out-of-workforce.html

Medline. (n.d.). Stress in childhood: Medlineplus medical encyclopedia. Retrieved February 2021, from https://medlineplus.gov/ency/article/002059.htm

Miller, K. (2021, January 19). 39 communication games and activities for KIDS, teens, and students. Retrieved February 2021, from https://positivepsychology.com/communication-activities-adults-students/

Paramapoonya, O. (2019, January 10). What are the causes of communication failure? Retrieved February 2021, from https://www.theclassroom.com/what-are-the-causes-of-communication-failure-12084449.html

Positive Parenting. (2021, March 15). How to get kids to (really) listen: 7 steps for success. Retrieved March, 2021, from https://www.positiveparentingsolutions.com/parenting/get-kids-to-listen

Schwarz, N. (2017, March 14). 5 reasons your kids don't talk to you (and how to change THIS PATTERN!). Retrieved February 2021, from https://imperfectfamilies.com/5-reasons-your-kids-dont-talk-to-you/

Sears, D. (2020, December 15). 25 ways to talk to kids so THEY LISTEN: ASK Dr. Sears. Retrieved February 2021, from https://www.askdrsears.com/topics/parenting/discipline-behavior/25-ways-talk-so-children-will-listen

WomensMedia. (2020, October 12). 10 steps to EFFECTIVE LISTENING. Retrieved February 2021, from https://www.forbes.com/sites/womensmedia/2012/11/09/10-steps-to-effective-listening/?sh=31d71cce3891

Wrike. (n.d.). 4 reasons why communication fails (and what to do about it). Retrieved February 2021, from https://www.wrike.com/blog/4-reasons-communication-fails/

Printed in Great Britain
by Amazon

60883245R00071